Northamptonshire PLACE-NAMES

EXPLORING THE HISTORY OF TOWNS, VILLAGES, STREETS & PUBS

■

Charles Whynne-Hammond

COUNTRYSIDE BOOKS
NEWBURY, BERKSHIRE

First Published 1994
© Charles Whynne-Hammond 1994

COUNTRYSIDE BOOKS
3 Catherine Road
Newbury, Berkshire

ISBN 1 85306 298 7

Designed by Mon Mohan

Illustrations by Glenys Jones

Map by Penny Veys

Produced through MRM Associates Ltd., Reading
Typeset by Paragon Typesetters, Queensferry, Clwyd
Printed in England

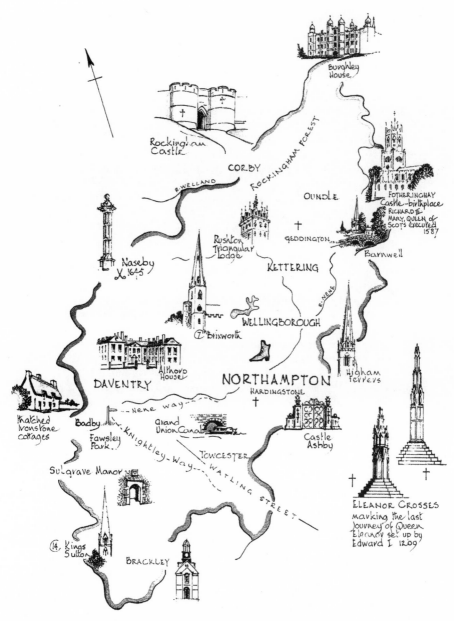

Burghley House

Rockingham Castle

CORBY

ROCKINGHAM FOREST

R. WELLAND

OUNDLE

FOTHERINGHAY
Castle - birthplace
RICHARD III
MARY, QUEEN of
SCOTS executed
1587

GEDDINGTON

Barnwell

Naseby
✕ 1645

Rushton
Triangular
Lodge

KETTERING

R. NENE

Brixworth

WELLINGBOROUGH

Althorp
House

Higham
Ferrers

DAVENTRY

NORTHAMPTON

HARDINGSTONE

Thatched
Ironstone
cottages

Badby

Grand
Union Canal

Castle
Ashby

Nene Way

Fawsley
Park

Knightley Way

TOWCESTER

WATLING STREET

Sulgrave Manor

ELEANOR CROSSES
marking the last
journey of Queen
Eleanor set up by
Edward I 1209

14 Kings
Sutton

BRACKLEY

© Map designed and drawn by PENNY VEYS 1994

Introduction

Ever since my university days I have been fascinated by place-names, their origins and meanings, the ways they have evolved and the links they have with nature. Place-names can tell us about the history of an area, the society of its former inhabitants and the geography of the landscape when it was first being settled. I have now lived in Northamptonshire for more than ten years and have grown to love its countryside, its subtle undulations, its thorny hedgerows, its broad meadows and wooded hillslopes. The villages are especially beautiful, constructed for the most part of honey-coloured lime-stone. They are quiet, unspoilt and undiscovered by the hordes of tourists that now descend upon the nearby Cotswolds.

The place-names of Northamptonshire are interesting because they are a mixture of Saxon and Viking elements – the Roman road of Watling Street, which bisects the county, once being the dividing line between Saxon England and Danelaw. They not only tell us how the Vikings changed the Saxon names but also tell us something of the landscape of the medieval Midlands, the extent of the forests, the breadth of the marshlands, the meanderings of the rivers. This book, I trust, conveys something of the fascination of place-names. Any omissions can be attributed to the limits of the size of the book. Any mistakes, I hope, can be forgiven since place-name study is a com-plicated subject. There are always new sources of information to be analysed and new ideas about linguistics to be considered.

I have enjoyed writing this book and hope you will enjoy reading it. I am grateful to the librarians, historians and county inhabitants who have helped my research. Rose and Peter Seery were especially helpful. I should like to thank Glenys Jones for her attractive selection of sketches and Gwen Cassell for her help in preparing the final draft.

Charles Whynne-Hammond
Rothwell, Autumn 1994

■ ABTHORPE

Thorpe, Thorp and Torp are common elements in English place-names, deriving from the Scandinavian word for 'village' or 'hamlet'. When the Vikings invaded England in the 9th and 10th centuries AD they moved into settlements formerly dominated by Saxons. In many cases they renamed those settlements, or else added a suffix like thorp or by (farmstead). In this case, the settlement was simply called Torp, and was so recorded in the Domesday Book in 1086. A century later it had become Abetrop, and by the 14th century Abethrop. The prefix was added to distinguish this place from other thorp villages. It comes from Abba, the name of a local tribal leader.

The little hamlet north-east of Abthorpe has a name derived from Fox Cot, but is now called **Foscote**. Cot usually meant 'cottage' in Saxon times but here probably meant 'burrow'.

Further south are **Hayes Farm** (probably derived from haeg, the Saxon word for 'enclosure') and **Challock Farm** (Charlock Farm) from the Saxon cald lacu (cold streamlet). A document of 1250 records Chaldelacke.

ADDINGTON, Great and Little

The Domesday Book (1086) records just a single settlement – Edintone. This became Edintune by 1348. In the following two centuries all sorts of spellings were used: Adinton, Adenton, Adynton, Adington and Adentona. The derivation was clearly from Eadda (a personal name), inga (the people of) and tun (farmstead). Thus, it was the farm where Eadda's people lived.

The pair of villages we know today are a good example of mother and daughter villages. As village populations grew during Saxon times and later, large overpopulated settlements used to set up colonial or daughter settlements nearby. These new villages would then keep the original name but add a distinguishing adjective, in many cases 'little'. Subsequently the mother village would add its own distinguishing adjective, 'great' perhaps, or 'much'. Here the 'Great' and 'Little' elements have appeared only since the 16th century. Before then other distinguishing adjectives were used. In 1287, for instance, Little Addington was called Adynton Waterville (after Hugh de Waterville who owned the manor) and in Tudor times

Great Addington was Nether Addington (as it was situated lower down the valley).

Between the two villages lies **Shooters Hill**. This was Scitershul in 1232 and Shetereshill in 1394. It was so called because archery practice used to take place here.

The old manor house, near the church in Great Addington, is not the original one. That is thought to have stood near the present **Home Farm**. From the 12th to the 16th century the estate was held by the de Vere family.

ADSTONE

Here, two different spellings were recorded in the 1086 Domesday Book: Atenestone and Etenestone. The origin is probably from Aettin's tun (farmstead). No doubt Aettin was a local tribal leader. By the 13th century the village had become Attelestuna; by the 14th century, Atteneston. In 1522 Adneston was recorded.

Some people have thought the suffix in this place-name has derived not from tun but from stone or stane – indicating the site of a long-lost boundary stone. Although such stones were indeed important in Saxon times – marking out land ownership rights – little evidence suggests that any boulders existed in this area.

ALDERTON

The first element in this name has nothing to do with alder trees, neither does it derive from earldormann, the Saxon word for 'alder-man'. In fact it comes from a personal name – Ealdhere, perhaps the name of a local leader. The second element derives either from ingtun (Saxon for farmstead) or else from inga – tun (Saxon words indicating a farm lived in by a group of people). So we have the meaning 'Ealdhere's farmstead' or 'the farm of Ealdhere's people'. In the Domesday Book the name was Aldritone, a century later, in 1184, Aldrinton. By 1283 it was Aldington.

ALDWINCLE

The spelling of this place name may have changed over the centuries, but its pronunciation seems to have remained the same. During the 11th century it was Aldewincla, Aldewyncle and Eldewincle; in the 12th century it was Aldewingel and in 1317 Aldwyncle. The derivation is probably from two Saxon words, ald (or eald) meaning 'old' and wincel meaning 'bend' or 'corner'. In this instance the latter is likely to have referred to a bend in the river Nene. Why such a bend should be called 'old' is a slight mystery. Perhaps the meanders of the river had already altered their course by the time the village was founded. It has been suggested that the prefix could have derived, instead, from Ealda (a personal name) or from alor (alder tree). However, neither origin can be supported by etymology.

This part of Northamptonshire was heavily forested once and still, today, many large woodlands survive. The name **Bradshaw Wood** was Bradehauw in 1293, a corruption of brad haga (broad enclosure). **Souther Wood** was Suthauwe in 1286, corrupted from south haga (southern enclosure).

Another interesting local name is **Brancey Bridge.** This was Brantsey in 1488, probably derived from Brant's eg, or ey, (island).

APETHORPE

This was Api's torp or throp (secondary settlement). Api is thought to be a Scandinavian personal name, and the torp was probably connected with the primary settlement of nearby King's Cliffe. In the Domesday Book it was Patorp (transposed Aptorp) but this changed to Apetorp (1162) and Apthorp (1281).

To the south is **Halefield Lodge**, which is a corruption of healh (nook or corner) and feld (open area of land) – hence, 'corner of a field'.

ARTHINGWORTH

This place-name derives from three separate Saxon elements but this does not necessarily mean that the village itself is Saxon in origin. The Saxon invaders might have settled in a village already founded by the Celts, and then merely changed the settlement's name into their own language. The three elements are Earna or Eardnoth (probably a personal name), inga (meaning 'people of') and worth (meaning 'enclosure'). Thus we have 'the homestead of the people of Earna'. In the Domesday Book it was Arniworde and Arningvorde; in 1181 Armingewerc; in 1202 Erningwrth. The present spelling dates from the 14th century.

However, it is interesting to note that the village stands on a hilltop site overlooking a river. Such was a favourite location for Celtic settlements during the Iron Age. In addition, Arthingworth has no fewer than nine tracks and roads radiating outwards, making it the hub of an ancient network of routeways. A site of antiquity indeed!

Nearby **Langborough Wood** was Langeberwe in medieval times, a corruption of long beorg (hill). **Waterloo Covert** has a much more recent origin however. It was named, of course, after the battle in 1815 when the Duke of Wellington finally defeated Napoleon.

ASHBY ST LEDGERS

Ashby is a very common place-name in England. It comes from the Saxon word aesc (ash tree) and the Viking word by (village). So common is it, however, that most villages that bear the name have in addition some distinguishing adjective: Great, Little, High or perhaps Cold (as found elsewhere in Northamptonshire). In this instance the identifying addendum comes from the dedication of its parish church, St Leger (otherwise Leodegar or Leodegarius). From the original Ascebi (11th century), Aissebi (12th century) and Essebi (13th century), the village became Esseby Sancti Leodegarii (in 1230) and Esschebi St Legers (in 1322).

Ashby St Ledgers is a pretty village which, for a period in Tudor times, was part of the estate owned by the Catesby family, one of whose number, Robert, was involved in the Gunpowder Plot.

Some of the old field names around the village are interesting.

Stadfield, for example, was once Stotfold (cattle enclosure) and **Woolspit** is a corruption of 'wolf's pit' – probably a snare to catch wolves.

ASHLEY

From Ascele in the Domesday Book (1086) and Estelai in 1109, this place-name acquired various spellings during the Middle Ages: Asshele, Assele, Asshelee, Asselee. It has a straightforward derivation, from the Saxon words aesc (ash tree) and leah (clearing in the wood).

During the 19th century the village was largely remodelled and contains some fine Victorian buildings. The rector, who was also the local squire, Richard Pulteney, commissioned Sir George Gilbert Scott (architect of London's St Pancras Station) to restore the church, and design the school together with a number of model cottages. Work finished in 1867.

ASHTON

Salcey Forest to the east and Whittlewood Forest to the south were once much larger than they are today, and indeed were only separated by the river Tove. So it should not be surprising that a village located in the midst of this area has a name derived from the Saxon words aesc (ash tree) and tun (farmstead). In the Domesday Book (1086) this village was Asce; in 1296 it was Asshen. The present name dates from the 16th century.

Other local names found in old documents include **Ashwood Farm**, which was Asshewode in 1337, and **Gun Hole**, which was Gunnildebrege (Gunnel Bridge) in the 14th century. The latter was probably a corruption of an Anglo-Scandinavian female name Gunhild.

ASHTON

Across the Nene meadows from Oundle this village stands close to an old Roman road. When it was first built, in Saxon times, it was set in a forest clearing. As with the previous entry the name – recorded in the Domesday Book as Ascetone – comes from aesc (ash tree) and tun (farmstead). Ash was a very useful tree to the Saxons, its timber being used for furniture and tools and its branches for basket-making. It was also a good source of fuel, since ash wood does not need to be seasoned before burning.

During the Middle Ages various spellings were used for this place name: Achestone, Ayston, Aiston, Aston and others. Nearby **Chapel Farm**, incidentally, is so called because Ashton was once a chapelry of Oundle, coming under the ecclesiastic jurisdiction of the Oundle parish.

This estate village is well known as the long-time home of Miriam Rothschild, wildlife expert and scientist. The name of the pub, **The Chequered Skipper**, is taken from a rare species of butterfly – one of many creatures this great conservationist helped save from extinction.

ASTCOTE

Just east of the old Roman road of Watling Street (now the A5) are three villages all with names ending in cote. This derives from the Saxon word cot meaning 'cottage'. Each settlement probably began life as an isolated farm set up by an individual who did not wish to live communally in a village perhaps because he was a stranger in the area or else because he was a freeman granted his own land.

Astcote was Aviescote in 1086 and is derived from Aefic's cot. Later it became Acheskot (1277) and Ascott (1542). Aefic is thought to have been a monk from Evesham to whom land at Newnham was given.

Eastcote was Edeweneskote in 1277 and is derived from Eadwine's cot. It became Edescote in 1404. The present name arose out of confusion with the original name, the village being east of Astcote.

Dalscote was Derstanescote in 1203 and is derived from Deorlaf's cot. In 1404 it was Derscote.

Westwards, beyond the A5 and near Cold Higham, is another -cote village: **Grimscote**. This is from Grim's cot.

ASTON-LE-WALLS

Interestingly, the 'le-walls' part of this name dates back only to Tudor times, yet it refers to a feature much older than the foundations of the village itself. For this addendum probably indicates the site of an old Roman vallum – an earth-made defensive embankment. This once ran for some 20 miles across the country from near Kirtlington. The first part of this name is from the Saxon east-tun meaning simply 'east farmstead'. This probably was a name relating to its position east of the Boddingtons. In the Domesday Book it was Eston; in 1200 Aston-Juxta-Wardon (next to Chipping Warden). Only in the 16th century did it become Assheton in the Walles.

The **Welsh Road**, or Lane, running across the northern edge of the village was an old drovers' road. This led from Wales to south-east England, via Buckingham, and was used by Welsh drovers taking their cattle and sheep to the English markets.

AYNHO

There have been various spellings of this name in the past, including Aienho in the Domesday Book, Aenho in the 12th century, Aieynho in the 13th century and Ayngho in the 14th century. The origin is thought to be from the Saxon Aega hoh. Aega was probably a local tribal leader and hoh meant a 'heel', a 'cliff' or a 'projection of land'. Hence it was 'Aega's ridge'.

Nearby **Smanhill Covert** was Smethenhulle in the 13th century, from the Saxon words smethe (smooth) and hyll (hill).

Pesthouse Wood, north-east of the village, commemorates the old pest house which stood amongst the trees. This was used to isolate plague victims. Villagers would leave food and drink for the inhabitants at the boundary fence.

College Farm is so called because of its long-time ownership by Magdalen College, Oxford.

The Cartwright family – lords of the manor from 1616 to 1954 – built many of the houses in Aynho and laid out many of its streets. In the 1820s William Cartwright named some of the thoroughfares for the first time. But this he did in a purely arbitrary way: Wapping,

Prospect Terrace, Paradise Row, Hart Lane, Spring Gardens. He also changed the name of the old coaching inn Red Lion to the **Cartwright Arms**. Many of the street names, however, are much older.

The Butts was an area where local archers had target practice during the late Middle Ages.

Hollow Way is so called because with constant use over many centuries it has been hollowed out and now runs in a narrow cutting.

Port Way is an ancient name for a market road. This lane once formed part of the main road from Souldern to Kings Sutton, used by locals going to market. Indeed, it was once the main Bicester to Banbury road, this particular stretch being bypassed in the age of the turnpikes.

■ BADBY

In the 1086 Domesday Book this was called Badebi but earlier had been known as Baddan Byrig and Baddan By. Originally it would have been Badda's Burh – the 'fort' or 'fortified place' belonging to a tribal leader named Badda. Burh was a Saxon word and the village was initially a Saxon settlement. After the Viking invasions, however, the new Scandinavian settlers changed this suffix to by, meaning in their language 'homestead' or 'village'. Without this change Badby might now be 'Badbury' or 'Badborough'.

It is not known if the burh in question was Arbury Hill, the nearby Iron Age hill fort. The name **Arbury Hill**, incidentally, is a corruption of the Saxon Earth-Byrig, meaning 'earthwork'.

The **Knightley Way**, the designated long-distance footpath from here to Greens Norton, is named after the family that once owned the Fawsley estate.

BARBY

Unusually for Northamptonshire this place-name could be wholly Viking in origin. Early versions of the spelling – Berchebi in the 11th century, Bewby in the 13th century, Berughby in the 14th century – suggest a derivation from the Scandinavian words berg (hill) and by (homestead, village). This does not necessarily suggest, however, that the village itself was first built by the Vikings. More likely the Norse invaders merely renamed an existing Saxon village.

To the west of Barby, hard by the Warwickshire border, is **Onley**. This was once a thriving village, called Onle in 1273 and Oneley in 1484. The name is a corruption of Ona's leah (clearing). Today Onley Fields and Onley Grounds preserve the name.

South-east of Barby is **Chapel Farm**. This is the site of a chapel thought to have belonged to Onley parish.

The **Arnold Arms** pub in Barby is named after a former lord of the manor. When the village was famous for the Barby Run, a race from Rugby School and back (as described in *Tom Brown's Schooldays*) the headmaster of that public school happened to be Thomas Arnold.

BARNWELL

The theory that this place-name comes from Bernes Well (children's well), and is associated with the ancient custom of dipping children into water, does not stand up to etymological study. More likely, it is a derivation from two Saxon words beorna (warrior) and wielle (spring). In the 11th century two spellings were used, Beornwelle and Bernewelle. Why a spring should be named after a warrior is not known. Perhaps warriors met here, or perhaps warriors used the spring water when defending the settlement against invaders. Barnwell Castle now stands on a knoll above the river, occupying a site long used by fighting men.

The castle is now the home of the Duke of Gloucester, a grandson of King George V. The pub in the village, **The Montagu Arms**, is so called from one of the Duke's family names.

Historically Barnwell was not one but two villages: Barnwell All Saints and Barnwell St Andrew. The church of the latter survives as the parish church, but that of the former has all but gone. Only the chancel survives. Inside are various memorials, including one to John Montagu, 4th Earl of Sandwich. He was the 18th century politician and gambler after whom the sandwich was named. At his club he used to order a slice of meat between two slices of bread, giving him a snack he could enjoy without leaving the gaming table.

To the south of Barnwell is **Wigsthorpe**, which was Wykingethorp in 1232 and Wigisthorp in 1428. This comes from Vikingr (Viking) and thorp (the Scandinavian word for 'village'). Apparently this was a community settled by the Norsemen.

BARTON SEAGRAVE

This village is separated from its larger neighbour, Kettering, by the **River Ise** and by the landscaped Ise Valley Park. The name Ise is ancient indeed, being of Celtic origin and related to the Sanskrit word udan meaning 'water'. In Saxon times this word became usion, which itself was connected with the name Ouse (a common English river name). In the 10th century the river Ise was the Ysan.

Barton Seagrave was simply called Berton in the Domesday Book and Bartone in 1179. This derived from the Saxon bere – tun meaning 'barley farm'. To distinguish itself from other Barton villages, the surnames of manorial owners were later added. In 1307 it was Barton Haurad (from William de Henred); in 1321, Barton Segrave (from Stephen de Seagrave).

The castle, whose remains and moat can still be seen west of the church and **Castle Way**, was built by Sir Nicholas Seagrave in the reign of Edward II.

Polwell Lane was originally called Polewell Lane, after a communal well, still to be seen in the post office garden. Its central pole is now missing. Nearby **Gotch Road** is named after Thomas Cooper Gotch, a well-known artist in Victorian times. His brother was the architect John Alfred Gotch, who was responsible for many local buildings.

BENEFIELD, Upper and Lower

The name that appears on documents before the Domesday Book – Beringafeld – gives an almost exact indication of its derivation. For it comes from three Saxon words: Bera (a personal name), inga (the people of) and feld ('open land' from which we get our modern word 'field'). Thus, it was 'the land of Bera's tribe'. By 1086 it had already changed to Benefeld, changing only slightly from then on, to include Banefeld in 1150 and Banifeld in 1230.

Only in the 15th century is the first mention of two separate villages: Benyfeld Netherthorp and Upthorpe ('lower farm' and 'upper farm' respectively).

BILLING, Great and Little

Once there was just a single village here called Belinge (in 1086) or Billynges (in 1156). This was derived from Bydel, a personal name, and inga meaning 'people of'. It is thought this village has an early Saxon foundation, perhaps going back to the 6th century. Two separate settlements appeared in the 13th century (Billinge Magna and Parva Byllinge) no doubt as a result of population growth. Magna became Great and Parva became Little in relatively recent times.

Billing Hall, in Great Billing, was built in 1776 and demolished in 1956. It was once owned by the Elwes family, now remembered in the **Elwes Arms** pub, **Elwes Way** and **Lady Winefride's Walk**.

Knights Court in Little Billing is named after the Knight family, which lived in the village for over 400 years. From their origins as farm labourers and thatchers the Knights became great local landowners.

BLAKESLEY

The river here is known as the Black Ouse but there is apparently no evidence that this gave us the name of the village. Early records give such spellings as Blaculveslei (1086), Blaculueslea (1185) and Blacoslegh (1330), all of which suggest an origin from Blaecwulf, a personal name, and leah, 'clearing'. In actual fact, it is most likely that the river name was taken from the village name, in what historians call a 'back formation'. In the 14th century, when the village was called Blakeslee, the river was called the Blakeslee Ouse.

The nearby village of **Woodend** was once called Little Blacolvesle (Little Blakesley), this later changing to Wood Blakesley.

The pub name **Bartholomew Arms** commemorates C W Bartholomew, who was the last lord of the manor, and a great local benefactor. Known as 'the Squire', he financed a rail connection between the hall and the main line station. He also helped to set up the town band. He died in 1919; his home, Blakesley Hall, was demolished in 1957.

Outside the village is a tree called **Dryden's Oak**. Tradition tells us that the poet John Dryden (who at one time lived at Blakesley) once took shelter here during a thunderstorm.

BLATHERWYCKE

During the 19th century this village was simply Blatherwick. The present spelling is a more recent embellishment. Early spellings varied: Blarewic (1086), Blatherewick (1242) and Blatherwygge (1391). The origin of this place-name is interesting, for the first element comes from the Saxon word blaedre or blather meaning 'bladder'. Bladder plants were commonly grown in Saxon England, cardamine, bladder-wort and bladder campion especially. They were highly regarded for their medicinal properties and were often grown on certain farms. Such was probably true in this case, since the suffix in the name comes from the Saxon wic, meaning 'specialist farm'.

To the south of Blatherwycke are **Cadge Wood** and **Hostage Wood**. The former name is possibly derived from an old word, cadge, used in falconry. The latter is thought to be a compound of haepse (Saxon for 'hasp' or 'fastener') and hecg (Saxon for 'hedge'). It was probably the site of a hedged enclosure which could be locked.

Another interesting old name in the vicinity is **Britain Sale**. This was Bryteyn Sale in the 16th century, named from the family of Ranulf Brito, who was granted a woodland here in 1227. The word Sale is either from the Saxon sealh (willow) or else from a local dialectic word for a division of land, or a 'woodland estate'.

Blatherwycke Hall, one-time home of the O'Brien family, the Earls of Stafford, was demolished in the early 20th century. The landscaped parkland, however, can still be seen.

BLISWORTH

This village boomed during the Industrial Revolution, becoming a centre for both canal and railway traffic. Indeed, so busy did the place become that pleasure gardens appeared close to the Blisworth Hotel and many famous music hall stars came up from London to perform. (The site is now a mobile home park.)

All this was a far cry from Blisworth's origins as a little Saxon hamlet set amidst the woodlands of Salcey Forest, then much bigger than it is today. In those days it would have been called something like Blioe's worth – the 'clearing' or 'enclosure' owned by a person called Blioe (or perhaps Bliohere). In the Domesday Book the name had become Blidesworde, and by 1166 it was Bliseworthe.

BODDINGTON, Upper and Lower

The spelling of this place-name in the Domesday Book (1086) was Botendon and a century later it was Bottendun. This suggests that the suffix comes not from the Saxon tun (farmstead) but from the Saxon dun (hill). The prefix derives from a personal name, thus giving us 'Bota's hill'. The middle syllable appeared in the 13th century, in the spelling Budinton, this later changing to Botyngdon. Either this came from the Saxon inga (people of) or was simply a euphonic inter-polation. Documentary evidence of two separate villages, Upper and Lower, comes only since the Middle Ages.

The **Welsh Road** running through Upper Boddington is part of the drove road from Wales to south-east England.

BOUGHTON

There are three possible origins for this name. Either it could come from a personal name, Bucca; or from the Saxon word boc (beech tree) or else from another Saxon word bucc (buck). With a suffix from tun, 'farmstead', we thus have three totally different meanings.

Sadly, neither etymological evidence nor historical information can tell us which of these three meanings is correct.

Early spellings of the name include Bochetone (1086), Bucton (1175), Bucketon (1394) and Bowghton (1597). No records have yet been discovered which mention a local tribal leader called Bucca (although this was a fairly common Saxon name), whilst our English forests were equally full of both beech trees and deer.

The **Whyte Melville** pub occupies the one-time home of Captain George Whyte-Melville, the author of sporting and historical novels who was also a great local philanthropist. He donated the royalties from his books to various good causes, including the establishment of working men's clubs.

Butchers Lane is named after an old butcher's shop that once stood next to the smithy.

BOZEAT

It was once imagined that this name comes from 'beau jet' – 'good spring'. Certainly there is a steady and pure jet of water here, and the name is indeed pronounced 'Bo-zhet', but no evidence exists to support this theory. More likely it is an origin from Bosa's geat (gate) – a gateway owned by a tribal leader. In the Domesday Book the place was recorded as Bosiete, this later changing to Bosegete (1155), Bosiate (1162) and Bosezate (1325). The gate might have been a meeting place for travellers – an entrance to a major routeway.

Throughout the Middle Ages the estate here passed through many owners: Matilda, daughter of Earl Waltheof, in the 11th century; the Bloet, Fitzpiers and Stokes families in the 12th century; the Haunford and Thivengh families in the 13th century and the Latimers thereafter until Tudor times.

In 1729 a great fire swept through the village, doing considerable damage. It began in what later became known as **Burnt Close**. At the end of that same century many new roads were laid out as a result of the Enclosure Act. Documents of the time name Harrold Road, Dytches Lane, Easton Lane, Turnpike Road, Bridle Road, Dog Lane and Stone Stile Lane.

Dyches later became **Dychurch**. It was once a ditch leading to the town well. **Top Road** and **Allan Hill** were once called Church End Road.

The **Dungee Woods**, to the east of Bozeat, were infamous for highwaymen in the 18th century and some think the name is a corruption of Danger Woods.

There is a house in the village that was once the home of Charles Spencelayh, the artist who specialised in painting Victorian house interiors.

BRACKLEY

From the early spellings of this name – Brachelai in 1086 and Braccalea in 1170 – it is not clear whether the prefix derives from a personal name like Bracca, or from the Saxon word braecen meaning 'bracken' or 'fern'. The derivation of the suffix is clear enough, however, from leah, 'woodland clearing'. The whole area was densely forested once and most settlements in this part of Northamptonshire began as small farmsteads in woodland clearings.

The small village of **Halse**, north-west of Brackley, was originally more important. It was Hasou in 1086, Halsou in the 12th century and Hausho in the 13th century. This name is thought to be a compound of the Saxon words heals (neck) and hoh (projecting ridge of land). The village stands on a ridge between two valleys.

The Old Town was the old Saxon centre of Brackley, clustering around St Peter's church. **St Rumbald's Well** is the place where, legend tells us, the saint preached a sermon within days of his birth. **Water Lane**, leading eastwards from here, was once an open ditch, carrying a stream to the Great Ouse meadows and to an old mill, where **Mill Lane** now runs. To the west of Old Town was once the old manor house, on the site of the Norman castle. It was burned down by the Royalists in 1645 and is commemorated by **Manor Road** and **Manor Court**.

Brackley grew substantially during the Middle Ages, at a time when much of the land hereabouts was owned by the Earls of Bridgewater and Magdalen College, Oxford. Many of the town's thoroughfares now recall these two great estates. **Bridgewater Road**,

Bridgewater Crescent, **Magdalen Meadows** and so on. The family name of the Bridgewaters was Egerton and this name is preserved in **Egerton Close**.

Other wealthy families which lived in Brackley in medieval times have also been remembered in street names: **Beaumont**, **De Quincey**, **De Montfort** and **Spencer** for example. **Waynflete Avenue** and **Close** recall William of Waynflete who bought lands here in the 15th century and established a school. **Soudan Avenue** comes from the family of Lawrence Soudan, who lived in the town in the 14th century.

More recent owners and inhabitants have also given their names to Brackley streets. The **Ellesmere estate,** east of Halse Road, remembers Lord Ellesmere who lived for a while in the High Street and owned much of the land north of the town at the beginning of the 20th century. He was also a great philanthropist. Numerous streets are named after former town mayors, and these include **Bannerman**, **Bartlett**, **Allen**, **Clarke**, **Coles**, **Hawkins**, **Gardener**, **Fenton**, **Cartwright**, **Stratton**, **Spiers**, and **Jones**.

Sadly many old street names have disappeared. **Halls Lane** was once called Blunts Lane, **Hill Street** was Tinkers Lane, **Buckingham Road**, Croft Lane and **St Peter's Road**, Old Town Lane. Other street names, fortunately, have survived. **Goose Green** was the original market square where poultry was sold. Nearby **St James Road** commemorates the old St James' chapel, once connected to the medieval hospital buildings.

On the north-western edge of town is **Flora Thompson Drive**. This is named after the author whose descriptions of country life in *Lark Rise to Candleford* caught the public imagination. As a child she lived at Juniper Hill (Lark Rise) and Cottisford, to the south of Brackley, on the Oxfordshire border.

Many of the pubs of Brackley also have interesting names. **Harrows** was previously called the Plough; the **Locomotive** stands next to the old bridge over the railway line – Brackley was once an important junction. **The Bell** is a common name throughout Northamptonshire. A bell was once the usual prize awarded to winners of steeplechase runs, in the early days of horseracing. In the 18th century horsemen used to race each other from church to church across the hedgerows – hence the modern word 'steeplechase'. **The Reindeer** is another common pub name hereabouts. The name refers, not to the Arctic reindeer, but to the hunted deer of 'tally-ho' sportsmen.

BRADDEN

From Bradene (1086) and Bradenden (1185) it is clear that the origin of this place-name is the Saxon brad – denu (broad valley). The village stands on a tributary of the river Tove.

The old name of **Bury Brake** nearby was mentioned in 1297 as Bury de Braddene. It was the burh (fortified place) near Bradden.

BRAFIELD-ON-THE-GREEN

The Domesday Book records two spellings, Brachefeld and Bragefeld, and a document of 1241 mentions Brafeld. The origin, it is thought, is Bragen feld. Bragen was the Saxon name for Yardley Chase and feld was the Saxon word for 'open tract of land'. Interestingly, on the far side of Yardley Chase, near Olney in Buckinghamshire, is another village called Brayfield. No doubt to distinguish these two places, adjectives were added during Tudor times. The village here in Northamptonshire became Brayfield de la Grene (as noted in 1503), while the other one became Cold Brayfield.

BRAMPTON ASH

This tiny village near the Leicestershire border was called simply Branton in the Domesday Book, becoming Bramton in 1203. The name derives from the Saxon words brame (brier, bramble) and tun (farmstead). Later on in the Middle Ages it was called Brampton-in-the-Ash to distinguish it from other Brampton villages. The village was once surrounded by ash woodland.

To the south lies **Hermitage Wood** and **The Hermitage**. The latter stands near the site of Hermitage House, demolished some time ago. Here once stood a chapel belonging to Pipewell Abbey, to which monks came for silent prayer. The main road in Brampton Ash is called **Hermitage Road** since it leads to that place.

BRAMPTON, Chapel and Church

Originally a single village stood here, called Brantone in the Domesday Book, Bramtone in 1194 and Bromton in 1215. The name is derived from the Saxon brame – tun (bramble – farm). As the population of the district grew, however, the village split into two. At first – during the early 13th century – these were called Little Brampton and Brampton Magna, but later the present names evolved. The Chyrche was first mentioned in 1287; the Chapell in 1474.

The **Spencer Arms** in Chapel Brampton was, from 1637 to 1824, an ale-house called the Stag's Head. The name was changed in 1825 when it became a public house (as opposed to an inn where lodging is provided). Like most of the village at that time, the pub was owned by the Spencer Estate, the Earls at nearby Althorp House. For most of the 19th century the place was famous as the venue for the Northamptonshire Farming and Grazing Society shows.

Hall Close occupies the site of old Brampton Hall, one-time home of the Dyve family (in the Middle Ages), the Treshams (in Tudor and Stuart times) and, more recently, the Gore family.

Eastwards across the river, beyond the site of an old ale-house called the Old Fish Inn, once stood the Pitsford and Brampton Railway Station, on the Northampton-Market Harborough line. This opened in 1859 and closed in 1981.

Just north of the station is **Spinney Farm**, once called Home Farm. This lies just below **Hoe Hill**, a name derived from the Saxon word hoh, 'spur of land'.

Merry Tom Lane, leading north-eastwards from here, is named after one of the first Earl Spencer's favourite hunters, killed while jumping a brook. The horse was buried close to where it fell, complete with saddle, stirrups and bridle. A memorial stone marks the spot.

BRAUNSTON

In the early 19th century this was a great trading centre, standing at the junction of the busy Grand Union and Coventry to Oxford canals. There were wharfs, moorings and numerous pubs, of which the **Boatman** survives as a reminder of those days of commercial water transport.

The village, however, goes back long before the years of 'canal mania'. It was called Brantestun in AD 956 and Brandeston in the Domesday Book (1086). Later spellings included Branteston (1175) and Braunston (1304). Whilst the suffix is evidently derived from tun (farmstead) there is debate about the origin of the prefix. Some people say it comes from a personal name, Brand or Brant; others suggest it is a corruption of the Saxon word brand meaning 'burnt'. Yet others suggest a derivation from brant meaning 'steep'. So it was 'Brand's farm'; a 'farm on land cleared by burning'; or a 'farm on a steep slope'.

Dark Lane runs down the canal-side to the spot known as Little Braunston. The name may come from the fact that it is a cul-de-sac, 'dark' in the sense of blind.

South of the village is **Berry Fields**. This was Beryfeld in 1540, being a corruption of Brandeston Bery. In medieval times there was a large manor house here, Bery being derived from bury or burh (fortified place).

BRAYBROOKE

This place-name is a corruption of the Saxon words brad (broad) and broc (brook), which may seem odd because the river here, the Jordan, is particularly small and narrow. Either the name arose out of irony or else, in Saxon times, the stream here was prone to frequent flooding.

In the Domesday Book the village was listed as Bradebroc. This later changed to Braibroc, Bradebroke, Brabroc and Breibroc.

The old castle here, built by lord of the manor Robert de Braybrooke, was demolished in the early 17th century. The farmhouse that replaced it was demolished in 1960. All that remains of either is the old farm brewhouse, and remnants of the old castle fishponds.

The **Swan Inn** was once called the Black Swan. It stands in **Griffin Road**. The Griffin family bought the castle from the Latymer family in Tudor times.

East of Braybrooke is **Eckland Lodge Farm**. This was Aiclund in 1199, a name probably derived from the Scandinavian words eik (oak) and lundra (wood).

BRIGSTOCK

Until recently it was thought that the prefix in this name came from the Saxon word brycg meaning 'bridge'. However, etymologists now think it comes, instead, from bierce, the Saxon for 'birch tree'. The suffix is derived from stocc (Saxon for 'stump' or 'log'). In the Domesday Book the spelling was Bricstoc, but later various other spellings appeared, including Bricestok, Brixstoke and Brikelstok. Although this name could have referred to a single stump – a birch trunk – it is more likely to have meant an enclosure surrounded by birch logs – a clearing ringed by a wooden fence. In this sense, the original settlement might have resembled a stockade.

At the centre of the village today is **Hall Hill**, where stands the war memorial. This was once the site of both the market place and a school, endowed by the Reverend Nicholas Latham in 1620.

Kennel Hill and **Stable Hill** commemorate the fact that Brigstock was once the home of the Woodland Pytchley Hunt. The stabling block built by Lord Londsdale towards the end of the 19th century has given way to a housing estate and the hunt now meets at Dingley. It was the same Lord Lonsdale, incidentally, who gave his name to the Lonsdale Belt, he being a sportsman and boxing enthusiast.

North of Brigstock, in Harry's Park Wood, is the **Bocase Stone**, marking the site of the Bocase Tree. This name probably derives from Bocas, a Saxon calendar event at which forest rights were handed out. The place became a meeting place and site for Saxon court hearings.

East of Brigstock is **Lyveden New Build**, a manor house left unfinished by the Tresham family in Stuart times. There was once a village here, called Louenden in 1175. This was a corruption of Leofa's denu (valley).

BRINGTON, Great and Little

Here we have a good example of mother and daughter villages. Originally there was just one settlement – called Brinintone in the Domesday Book and Brunton in 1248. Then, as the population grew, that village set up a colonial settlement nearby to house the overspill. The older, original, village then acquired a distinguishing adjective (Great) while the younger, newer village added its own distinguishing name (Little). Here the place-name derives from Bryni's tun (farmstead). In 1330 we find Brynkton; the separate names appearing some time later.

During the 19th century this area was largely incorporated into the Althorp Estate. **Althorp House**, home of the Earls of Spencer, stands close to the site of a Saxon hamlet called Olletorp in 1086 and Olthorp in 1208. This derived from Olla (a personal name) and thorp (settlement).

On the estate is the name **Chinkwell**, referring to a belt of trees. This name probably arose because there was a wielle (spring) in a chink in the ground (that is, a hollow). To the south of here is **Nobottle** a corruption of the Domesday Book name Neubote, meaning 'new building'.

To the west of Great Brington is **Moor Farm**. This takes its name from Roger de la More, who owned the land in the 13th century. South of here is **Gawburrow Hill**. This is a corruption of the Saxon words cald (cold) and beorg (hillock or burial chamber).

BRIXWORTH

The origin of this name is Bricel's worth, Bricel being the name of a local tribal leader and worth being Saxon for 'clearing' or 'enclosure'. In the Domesday Book the spelling was Briclesworde, in the following century this becoming Brihteswthe. Later, in 1421, it was Brekelesworth.

Brixworth is the home of the Pytchley Hunt, whose kennels are just north of the village. The Tudor dated hall – now demolished – was for many years owned by the Saunders family.

The **Coach and Horses** pub is well named. It was once a famous coaching inn, on the road from London to the north.

During the 19th century the village grew as an industrial centre and much evidence still remains of this period. There were iron ore works, a railway station and a workhouse.

Evidence of an earlier period can be found south-east of the village where an old field name **Wolfage Piece** recalls a long-gone estate called Wolfhegge in the Middle Ages. That name meant 'wolf hedge' – probably an enclosure to keep out wolves.

BROCKHALL

Once a much larger village, this is now just a hamlet in the centre of an estate parkland. The hall was built in the early 17th century by the Eyton family but from 1625 to 1978 was the home of the Thornton family.

The early spellings – Brocole in 1086, Brochole in 1220 and Brockhole in 1316 – clearly indicate a derivation from the Saxon words brocc (badger) and hol (hole). It was probably named after a badgers' set. Interestingly, 'Brock' has become the traditional name for a badger.

BROUGHTON

'First mentioned in the Domesday Book as Burtone, this name derives from the Saxon words broc and tun meaning 'stream' and 'farm' respectively. In 1125 it was Brohtune and in 1275 Broghton. It is from the word broc, of course, that we get our modern word brook.

Apart from agriculture the village has, in the past, depended upon the shoe industry, iron workings and a little lace-making. Broughton is also well known for the custom of the Tin Can Band, when, one night in December, locals traditionally scare away gypsies by parading through the streets with whistles, trumpets and tin cans.

BUGBROOKE

From Buchebroc and Buchebroch in the 11th century, and Boogbrooke in 1595, we can surmise that this name comes directly from the Saxon words bucc (buck) and broc (stream). Deer were common in the forests of Dark Age England, and this stream could have been a spot where stags gathered to drink.

The **Bakers Arms** pub stands on the site of an old bakehouse. **Campion School** is so named after a much respected local resident and farmer. On the northern edge of the parish is a spot called **Knitters Grave**. This was named after a certain Richard Knitter who committed suicide whilst awaiting trial for murder. Legend says he was buried here in non-consecrated ground beyond the parish boundary.

BULWICK

This village name had various spellings through the Middle Ages, but it was probably always pronounced as it is today – 'Bullick'. Early documents record Bulewic, Bolewyk, Bulwic, Bulwyk and Bollewyk, amongst others. The origin is from the Saxon bula – wic (bull – farm). Perhaps the settlement began as a specialist beef-producing farmstead.

In the early Middle Ages the estate was owned by Reginald Fityurse, one of the four knights who murdered the 'turbulent' priest Thomas à Becket in 1170. More recently Bulwick Hall was owned by the Tryon family.

Another village once existed nearby called **Henwick**, but this disappeared as a result of plague and the enclosure of farmlands in medieval times. That name was a corruption of henn-wic (hen-farm).

BURTON LATIMER

This was simply Burtone in 1086 and Birton in 1230, derived from the Saxon burh (fortified place) and tun (farmstead). No doubt it was a defensive settlement. In the late 13th century the manor was held by William le Latymer and subsequently his name was added to the village name. In 1482 we find Burton Latymer.

Outside the town are **Buccleuch Farm** and **Harper's Lodge**. The Dukes of Buccleuch of Boughton House, near Kettering, have long held lands in this area, and John Harper held the Burton Latimer estate during the 18th century.

BYFIELD

Situated close to the Warwickshire border this has long been a busy, industrious settlement. During the Middle Ages it was a drovers' centre (being situated near the **Welsh Road** drover's route from Wales to south-east England) and boasted an important cattle market at **Fiveways** (named from the five roads joining there). Later, after the Industrial Revolution, it acquired an ironstone quarry, a boot and shoe industry and a railway station, all of which caused the village to spread out, incorporating the once separate village of **Westhorpe** (west thorp or settlement).

Originally Byfield was Bifelde (in 1086), a name which simply meant 'by the forest clearing' or 'by the open land'. In 1121 it was Bifeilt.

The pub called the **Cross Tree** (formerly the New Inn) is named after the cross tree in the High Street. The present one is an oak planted in 1979 but the original was planted in 1753 to mark the site of the old stone cross where medieval buying, selling and bartering took place. The pub still holds an interesting auction every year, based on the old land letting ceremony.

Many of the street names recall former inhabitants and philan-thropists. **Thomas Close** and **Edwards Close** are named after Thomas Edward of Bugbrooke who left money to the village when he died in 1725. **Fessey** remembers Joseph Fessey, who left £1,200 to the poor in 1897; and **Lovett Road** recalls John Lovett who gave £150 in 1934 to buy coal for the impoverished. **Knightley Close** is named after Sir John Knightley, rector of Byfield 1777-1810 who left money for the Sunday school, whilst **Greenwood Close** recalls the Greenwood Charity, established in 1693. **Becketts' Close** and **Potters End** are named after two former landowners, and **Jubilee Close,** opened in 1936, after the Silver Jubilee of George V and Queen Mary. **Muddy Lane** was once called Pot Lane – site of an old rubbish tip.

■ CANONS ASHBY

The original name Ascebi (in 1086) simply meant 'farmstead by the ash tree', from the Saxon word aesc (ash) and the Viking word by (farmstead or village). Soon after the Normans had secured their hold over England, however, a priory was founded here and the name changed. Stephen de Leye founded the priory in the 12th century for 13 canons of the Augustinian order. Soon after, the village became known as Canounes Hessheby, this changing by the 13th century to Essheby Canons and Assheby Canonicorum. In 1506 we find Chanons Assheby.

At the Dissolution of the monasteries the priory estates were acquired by Francis Bryan. Later they passed to the Cope family, thence to the Dryden family (one of whose number was John Dryden the poet).

Outside the village are two interesting old names. **Conduit Covert** was so called because pipes used to take water from ponds nearby to the priory, thus supplying the canons with drinking water. **Wards Copse** was named after the family of John le Ward, who owned land here.

CASTLE ASHBY

Like other villages called Ashby this derives from the Saxon word aesc (ash tree) and the Scandinavian word by (farmstead or village). In the Domesday Book it was simply called Asebi, this changing to Esseby and Axeby in the 13th century.

During the 14th century the manor was held by David, Earl of Huntingdon and for a while the village was known as Assheby Davey. Later that same century, however, it was recorded as Castel Assheby in which name it remained. Castle Ashby House, on the site of the original castle, is owned by the Compton family, the Marquesses of Northampton (who also own Compton Wynyates in Oxfordshire).

The nearby hamlet of **Chadstone** was Cedestone in the Domesday Book, deriving from Ceadd's tun (farm). Ceadd could have been a tribal leader.

CATESBY, Upper and Lower

A wholly Viking name this, coming from a Scandinavian personal name, Kati or Kate (perhaps a local tribal leader) and the Viking word by (village or farmstead). In 1086 it was Catesbi, later becoming Katesby and Cattesbi. The separate villages of Upper and Lower Catesby appeared in the late Middle Ages. The former developed around a 12th century nunnery that once stood here.

There are several place-names of Saxon origin in the vicinity suggesting the area was not entirely settled by Vikings. **Dane Hole** is from denu (valley); **Ryton Hill** is from ryge (rye) and dun (hill) and **Steppington Hill** is from steap (steep) and dun. **Catwell Barn** is a corruption of cattle well.

CHACOMBE

Up to fairly recently the spelling Chacombe and Chalcombe were equally used, but the former is closer to the early spellings. These include Cewecumbe (in 1086) and Chaucumba (1176). The name comes from Ceawa's cumb (valley).

The village stands on the border with Oxfordshire and once had an important cloth industry, as suggested by such cottage names as **Weavers**. **Bell Cottage** stands on the site of the old Bagley Bell Foundry, which stood here from 1600 to 1785.

Silver Street was once called Saucepan Alley and **School Hill** was Upper Tubs. The road to Banbury boasted the name Catchall.

CHARLTON

In Saxon times most farmworkers who did not own land were tied to particular estates, employed as indentured labourers. A few, however, achieved freeman status and were able to work for themselves on land they had been granted. Such people were called ceorls. And it was these people who gave their name to this settlement – ceorls' tun (a farmstead being run by ceorls). In the Domesday Book (1086) it was called Cerlintone, in 1247 Chorlton and in 1316 Charleton.

To the west is **Newbottle** now a hamlet but once more important than Charlton. This was Neubote in 1086 and Neubotl in the 12th century – from niwe – bothl (new building).

Charlton was the home, until his death in 1930, of F.E. Smith, the lawyer and statesman who became Lord Chancellor and the first Earl Birkenhead.

CHARWELTON

This was once known as Upper Charwelton, and the hamlet a little to the south-east (now called Church Charwelton) was known as Lower Charwelton. And it was the latter which is referred to in the Domesday Book as Cerweltone. This became Charwalton by the 12th century.

The village grew up as the tun (farm) on the river Cherwell, which today rises in the vicinity of Cherwell House. But in the 14th century the Black Death decimated the population and the village fell into a decline from which it never recovered. At about the same time the line of the main road was changed, so the few inhabitants that remained moved to a new settlement, which became known as Upper Charwelton.

Today Charwelton is quiet. The Great Central Railway, which arrived in 1897, has gone, and with it the little industrial base that the place once enjoyed. The old school donated by the Knightleys of Fawsley closed in 1935.

Foxhall Farm was once a coaching inn, but the **Fox and Hounds** has successfully survived as a pub since the 17th century.

CHELVESTON

This derives from a personal name, Ceolf or Ceolwulf, and the Saxon word tun (farmstead). It was Celuestone in the Domesday Book and Chelfiston in 1262.

Nearby **Caldecott** was Caldecote in 1086 and this was a corruption of ceald (cold) and cot (cottage). Either the cottages themselves were cold – built humbly and with poor materials – or else they were positioned in a cold location. Certainly this part of east Northamptonshire suffers from cold winds off the North Sea, so either case is likely.

CHIPPING WARDEN

Chipping is an interesting place-name element. It comes from the old Saxon word cieping meaning 'market', itself derived from ceap meaning 'to barter'. From the same root we get our modern street name Cheapside and our word cheap. Chipping did not appear in this place-name, however, until the 14th century: Chepyng Wardoun is recorded in 1389. Before then it was simply Waredon (1086) and Wardon (1163), from the Saxon words weard (watch) and dun (hill). The village was evidently named from a local look-out point (Warden Hill nearby).

The Griffin pub is named after the lords of the manor during the 15th and 16th centuries, It was originally located on the main road, at a site now occupied by the house called The Beeches.

CLIPSTON

Various spellings are found in medieval documents: Clippeston, Clypston and Clypson as well as Clipestune (the one found in the Domesday Book). It is thought the prefix comes from a Scandinavian personal name, Klyppr: hence Klyppr's tun (farmstead).

In the surrounding countryside other old names have interesting origins. **Longhold Lodge** was Longwoldes in the 13th century, from long weald (woodland). **Nobold Farm** was Neubold in the 14th century, from niwe (new) and bothl (building). **Twantry Farm** was Twantr in 1381, possibly a corruption of twaem – treowum (at the two trees).

CLOPTON

This village is also known as Clapton, but Clopton is closer to its original spelling, the earliest record of which is dated about AD 960. Then it was Cloptun which meant 'stump farm', 'hill farm' or 'rock farm' – 'clop' having various meanings in Saxon times. In the Domesday Book the name is given as Clotone and in 1227 Clapton.

The old and unusual name **Long Thong Farm** nearby was Langetuang in the 13th century, deriving from the Saxon word thong meaning 'a strip of hide or leather'. In this case the word probably applied to the shape of a piece of land.

Ringdales Wood has locally been known as Ringsdon Wood, perhaps indicating its derivation from ring (round) dun (hill). Closer to the village is another woodland, this one called **Skulking Dudley Copse**. The Dudleys were lords of the manor. In 1349 a member of that family was accused of murder. The story goes that this accusation so unhinged the nobleman's mind that he became furtive and morose, thus gaining the nickname Skulking Dudley. It is said his ghost still wanders between Clopton and nearby Barnwell.

COGENHOE

This name is pronounced 'Cooknoe', which gives less indication of its derivation than its spelling. It comes from the Saxon words cucken (to spy) and hoh (hill). The village is set high up above the Nene Valley and must once have been an excellent look-out point. In the Domesday Book (1086) it was Cugenho, but later became Cugeho (12th century), Cuggenho (13th century) and Cokenalle (16th century).

COLD ASHBY

This is the highest village in Northamptonshire. Situated at 700 feet above sea level, on the crest of the hills which are a continuation of the Cotswolds, it is perhaps no wonder that it has gained the place name element 'cold'.

In 1086, at the time of the Domesday Book, it was known simply as Essebi (from aesc meaning 'ash tree' and by meaning 'village' or

35

'homestead'). But confusion with other Ashby villages in the county led to the first element being added fairly soon afterwards. By 1150 it was Caldessebi.

Two local names of interest are **Chilcote's Cover** and **Portly Ford Bridge**. The former is a corruption of the Saxon cild-cot (a cottage inhabited by young men or servants) and the latter is a corruption of Portway (an old name for a main road, or a route that led to a market).

COLD HIGHAM

The present name only goes back to the 16th century when it was spelt Cole Higham. Before then it was just Hecham (as in 1086) or Hegham (as in 1316). That was a corruption of heah (high) and ham (homestead). The village stands on raised ground. It was on an exposed position, a fact that led to its present adjectival element.

Nearby **Grimscote** was Grimescote and Grimmescot in the Middle Ages – a corruption of Grim's cot (cottage). **Potcote**, also close by, was once a cottage in a hollow.

COLLINGTREE

This was once 'Cola's tree', from the name of a Saxon tribal leader and the Saxon word treow. In the Domesday Book (1086) it was recorded as Colentreu, this later changing to such spellings as Colintrie (1162), Colyngetre (1322) and Colyngtrough (1367). The 'tree' in question might have been of some special significance in Cola's time. Perhaps it marked a boundary between estates; or it could have been a religious site; or perhaps even the spot where gatherings and meetings took place.

The manor house was owned, during the 19th century, by the Phipps family, which ran a brewing company. There was once a brewery in the village.

COLLYWESTON

This was originally the west tun (farm) in relation to Easton-on-the-Hill, which lies to the east. In the Domesday Book it was called Westone. In the 14th century, however, the estate passed into the hands of Sir Nicholas de Segrave and the name was expanded to include the name of this new owner. Since, in Norman times, Colyn was the pet name or diminutive for Nicholas the village became Colynweston (as recorded in 1309) and Colyn's Weston (as recorded in 1331). The present spelling was first used in 1575.

The medieval mansion of Collyweston Palace was demolished in 1640. Having been a royal possession (owned by Henry VII and given by Henry VIII to Anne Boleyn) it had passed down to the Tryon family. Today much of the area is owned by the Burghley Estates Trust.

The **New Road** at the bottom of the High Street is so called because it was new when it was built – in 1650. It was constructed to link the village with the recently built bridge over the river Welland.

Deepside runs along the edge of an area called The Deeps. Now a conservation area, this was once a stone quarry where roofing slates were cut. Collyweston slates are widely famous for their quality. The **Cavalier** pub in Main Street was so named in 1973. Before then it was the Slaters' Arms.

CORBY

Corby may be a New Town now but its name goes back 1,000 years to the time of the Viking invasions. Originally it would have been Kori's by – the 'farmstead' or 'village' of a Scandinavian tribal leader called Kori. In the Domesday Book it was Corbei and 80 years later, in 1166, it was Corebi. The original settlement was no more than a hamlet in the midst of Rockingham Forest. Its position was probably where Old Town now centres on the High Street and **The Jamb**. The latter has an interesting derivation: it is thought to be a corruption of the French word 'jambe' meaning 'leg'. The Normans might have called it this because of its then dog-leg shape; The Jamb was the place, in medieval times, where the old Pole Fair took place.

One of the oldest pubs in the town is the **Knights Lodge**. This dates from the 17th century and was originally a lodging house used by knights who went hunting in the surrounding forest. It is said to be haunted by no less than four ghosts – a cowled monk, a cavalier and two children.

Corby remained a small settlement, surrounded by woods and farm-land, up to the Industrial Revolution. Some of the area names reflect this rural past: Hazel Leys, Beanfield, Kingswood, for example. Others reflect former landowners – and here Exeter is a good example. One of the great landowners in north-east Northampton-shire has long been the Lords Burghley, the Marquess of Exeter family. In the 17th century the manorial estate passed from the Hatton family of nearby Kirby Hall to the Brudenell family (the Earls of Cardigan) of Deene Park.

The beginnings of industrialisation came with the handloom weaving trade, closely followed by the opening of the brickworks in the early 19th century. But it was the coming of the railway line in 1879 that had the most devastating effect upon the town. For it was the cutting of the land by the railway company that caused the discovery of ironstone deposits.

Lloyds Road recalls the Lloyds Ironstone Company, one of the first companies to move into the town in the 1880s. At first iron ore was dug here and transported to the west Midlands for smelting but in 1910 the first blast furnaces were built locally. Lloyds became Stewarts and Lloyds in 1920, their major steel and tube works moving to Corby in the early 1930s. The first 'Bessemer' steel was cast here in 1934. The modern new town was instigated after the Second World War and urban growth has continued ever since.

Some of the old names in the area have survived however. **Great** and **Little Excellent** is a corruption of Great and Little Exland, derived from the Saxon word exen, the plural of 'ox'. Hence this was 'oxen-land'.

Stockey Wood was once called Stockerwood, from the Saxon word stocc for 'trunk' or 'stump'. Thus, we have a meaning of 'wood of stumps' – possibly a recently felled area of forest. **Occupation Road** is on the site of Occupation Farm, an estate held by a tenant farmer. Just east of this is **Pengreen Lane**. There was once a Pen Green Lodge here (first recorded in the 17th century). It is thought 'pen' is a corruption of the Saxon word penn meaning 'enclosure' or 'animal pound'. Incidentally, the road names around Pen Green commemorate some of the great men of the Industrial Revolution: George and Robert Stephenson, Thomas Telford, James Watt and others.

COSGROVE

It is hard to imagine that Cosgrove – now so close to Milton Keynes – was originally set amongst the trees of Whittlewood Forest. It was Cufel's graf (grove), a village situated in a wooded clearing and owned by a Saxon called Cufel. In the Domesday Book it was Covesgrave, in 1275 Cosegrave.

During the Industrial Revolution Cosgrove grew as an important canal town, and much evidence still survives of those busy days.

The old priory has been owned by three great families in the past: the Mansells, the Thorolds and the Atkinsons. Behind the old National School is **St Vincent's Well**, a holy well famed during the Middle Ages for its healing qualities. Its water was thought to cure eye infections.

COTON

Cota in the Domesday Book and Cotes in the 14th century derived simply from cot, the Saxon word for 'cottage'. 'Cote' or 'cot' is a common element in place-names so – to distinguish one village from another – it is often linked with another element. Holcot (cottage in a hollow), Muscott (mice cottage), Astcote (Aefic's cottage) and so on. Coton, however, is different and has no appendage. This has not always been true, for it was known for a while in the Middle Ages as Cotene juxta Gildeburg (cottage next to Guilsborough).

To the north-west, near Yelvertoft, is **Clay Coton**. This was Cotes in 1175 and Cleycotes in 1284, so named because it was sited on heavy clay soil.

COTTERSTOCK

This was Codestock in the Domesday Book, Cothestoche in the 12th century and Coderestoke in 1253. This name is thought to derive from the Saxon words corther (troop, assembly or band) and stoc (place). The settlement was evidently the site of public gatherings.

The 12th century church once had a college adjoining, founded by John Gifford in 1338. It was a religious establishment and so lasted only until the Dissolution in 1536. Close to the mill was once a river wharf, serving the town of Oundle a little upstream.

COTTESBROOKE

In this case the prefix probably does not come from the Saxon word cot (cottage) but from a Saxon personal name – Codd. Thus we have the meaning 'Codd's stream' rather than 'cottage by the stream'. The Saxon word broc obviously has given us our modern word brook. In the Domesday Book the village was Codesbroc, in 1332 Catesbrok. The present spelling first appeared in 1639.

To the north of the village is **Mitley Spinney**. This was Mittelowehul in the Middle Ages, originally meaning 'middle hill'.

Westwards is **Calender Farm**. This is a corruption of Kayland. There was once a small religious house here – Kayland's Cell – founded in 1150 by monks linked to the order of St Norbert, based in Laon in France. Known also as the White Canons this order lasted until Henry VIII's Dissolution of the Monasteries. Near Hinsons Meadow there is also a field called **St Norberts Field**, in which is **Monk's Well**.

COTTINGHAM

There is more than one possible derivation to this name. Either it might come from cot (cottage), inga (people of) and ham (farmstead), or else it could be from Cotta (a personal name) and ingham (settlement or main homestead). There are some etymologists who think the suffix could even be derived not from ham but from hamm (meadow). Whatever the exact meaning originally, the name is clearly Saxon. In 1086 it was Cotingeham and in 1162 Cottingeham.

Great Cattage Wood, nearby, was Catteheggis in the 15th century and Cathege in the 16th century. These derived from catt (wild cat) and hege (hedge). Evidently there was a hedged enclosure here, constructed to keep out wild cats.

COURTEENHALL

This attractive hamlet, close to the M1 motorway, is set in the middle of a landscaped estate. The Hall has been owned by the Wake family since its construction in 1791. After the Domesday Book, when the name was given as Cortenhale, various spellings were used, including Curtehala, Cortehalle, Corthala and Corinhall. It derives from Corta's healh (nook of land).

CRANFORD

Actually there are two villages here: Cranford St Andrew and Cranford St John, each being recognised by the dedication name of its parish church. They are divided by the Alledge brook. They have a common early history, the present distinction in place and name being a fairly recent phenomenon. In the Domesday Book (1086) we find, simply,Craneford. This later became Cranesford and Cranneford. The place was, literally 'crane's ford' – the ford where cranes or herons were seen.

For a short while – in the 13th century – the village was called Esseby Cranford due to the fact that the manor was held by William de Esseby.

It is not uncommon for a single village to become, in time, two separate villages. Sometimes the original settlement set up a colonial or daughter settlement; sometimes villagers moved to a more favourable position, towards a newly routed main road for example.

CRANSLEY, Great and Little

Great Cransley is the older of these two, the first element not being added until Tudor times when Little Cransley appeared. Before then we simply had Cranesleg (as recorded in the Domesday Book). The earliest spelling so far discovered dates from AD 956: Cranslea Bricg

(Cransley Bridge). Whilst the prefix is clearly from the Saxon cran (crane or heron) there is some dispute about the origin of the suffix. Either it comes from the Saxon eg (island) or from the Saxon leah (clearing).

The **Three Cranes** pub recalls the coat of arms belonging to the former manorial owners. Cranes also appear in the church's stained glass window.

CREATON

Strictly speaking this is Great Creaton. There is a Little Creaton a short distance to the south. The two settlements were first mentioned in the 13th century, as Magna and Parva, after population growth had caused the original village to split into a mother and daughter pairing.

That original settlement was called Craptone and Cretone in the 11th century and Cratton in 1285. The suffix clearly comes from tun, the Saxon word for 'farmstead', but there is debate about the derivation of the prefix. It could either be taken from a personal name, Crec or Creic, or else be a corruption of the village name of Crick (some distance to the west). Some etymologists have also suggested that the origin could be much older, being derived from an ancient Celtic word craig or cruc meaning 'rocky hill'.

The **Horseshoe Inn** was so named because there was once a landlord who had been a blacksmith. In the 1960s a fire badly damaged the building soon after it had been rethatched. The **Bricklayers Arms** was built just before the First World War, and just after the local brickworks had closed down.

CRICK

If this name were of Saxon origin it would probably derive from cerrig meaning a 'crag' or 'rocky outcrop'. If, on the other hand, it were Viking in origin it would probably come from kreik meaning a 'narrow inlet' or 'stream' (as in our modern word 'creek'). Etymologists have not yet agreed although the situation of the village – on a small limestone hillock – suggests the first option is the more likely.

The pronunciation of this place-name has not changed much over the years although the spellings have. In the Domesday Book it was Crec. Later came Kreic, Creke, Creek and Kreke all during the 13th and 14th centuries.

Lauds Road is named after Archbishop Laud, who was martyred for his Catholic beliefs in 1645. He was once rector here. **Boat Horse Lane** was the route taken by canal horses, whilst their narrow boats and barges were 'walked' through the tunnel housing the Grand Union Canal. Since no towpath existed, boatmen had to lie on their backs and 'walk' along the tunnel roof, thus propelling their vessels along.

There are two house names of interest in Crick. **Phoenix House** in the High Street was built in the 19th century entirely of blue bricks left over after the building of the Kilsby railway tunnel. The phoenix was the mythical bird that rose from its own ashes. **Queen's House**, in Lauds Road, was originally called 'The Cabin'. It was given by Queen Victoria to George Smith, the Coalville-born preacher and philanthropist who had made his fortune from pottery and brick manufacture.

CROUGHTON

The Domesday Book listed no fewer than three spellings for this village name: Creveltone, Criweltone and Cliwetone. It seems most likely that the origin was creowel (fork) tun (farmstead). In Saxon times creowel was a word most often applied to a river fork – where two streams met or a single stream divided. Later spellings included Creulton (1174), Creueltune (12th century) and Crouleton (13th century).

Rowler, or **Rowler's Farm**, to the north of Crick towards Brackley, was called Roulowe in the 13th century. This derived from the Saxon ruh (rough) and hlaw (hill). **College Farm** was so called because of its ownership by Magdalen College, Oxford.

CULWORTH

This was Culeorde in 1086 (Domesday Book) and Culewurda in 1184, from the Saxon personal name Cula and worth meaning 'enclosure'. In the 13th century it was Colewyth, in the 14th century Collewrth. One part of the village had the separate name Cote Culworth in the 16th century (meaning 'cottage Culworth') but this has not survived.

Berry Hill – **Berry Close Hill** – is believed to be the site of a Norman castle, built during the reign of King Stephen (in the 12th century). The name comes from the Saxon burh (fortified place or fort). Not far away is **Fulford Farm**. This was Fulebroc in the Middle Ages, from ful (muddy) and broc (stream).

Wadground Barn, to the north-west was woad ground in 1771. Woad (from the Saxon word wad) was grown in this area, a plant used in the making of dyes.

In the 18th century Culworth was the base for the notorious Culworth gang of outlaws. Today, however, all is quiet. In the wall of the old school is a boulder called **King Charles' Pebble**. It is said that King Charles I mounted his horse from this rock, when he was taking refuge here during the Civil War.

■ DAVENTRY

The old spelling Danetre, and pronunciation 'Daintry', once led people to think this name derived from 'Dane tree' – and indeed, the town's seal actually shows a Dane felling a tree. But this origin has been disproved. So also has the alternative suggestion that the name is a corruption of the old Celtic words dwg – afon – tre meaning 'the homestead of the two rivers'. In fact the origin is probably from the name of a Saxon tribal leader, Dafa and the Saxon word treo (tree). Whether this personal name was taken from a local river, or from a word meaning 'fitting', is not known. The 'tree' in question could have been a religious marker (a wooden cross), a focal point for meetings, or a boundary mark.

In the Domesday Book the spelling was Daventrei and in 1216 it was Daivintre. The old pronunciation of the name is preserved in the local names **Daintry Wood** and **Daintree Farm**.

Drayton, to the north-west of the town centre and now a suburb, has an interesting derivation. Recorded as Draiton and Dreyton in the 13th century, it comes from the Saxon words draeg and tun. The latter meant 'farmstead' but the former was a word used by the Saxons to describe a particular feature in the landscape. It originally referred to a narrow strip of land or an island over which boats were pulled from one river to another. Our modern word 'drag' comes from the same root. In due course any area where timber was dragged along was called a draeg.

All around Daventry old names can be traced back through early documents. **Borough Hill**, for example, was once called Borow Hill and derives from the Saxon word burh meaning 'fortified place' or 'fort'. It is the site of an Iron Age hill development.

Just south of there is **Burnt Walls**, which was Les Brendewalles in 1255. Old foundations have been discovered that suggest that some ancient buildings may actually have been burned down.

North of Daventry is **Middlemore Farm**. This was Micklemoor in the 18th century, a name taken from old Saxon Micelmor meaning 'big marsh' or 'large pool'.

Hackwood Farm was so called because trees had been felled to make a clearing (hacked wood); **Fousill Wood** was Foweleswellehul originally, from fugol (bird) wielle (spring) and hyll (hill); **Stepnell Spinney** was Stepenhul, from steap (steep) and hyll (hill); **Falconershill** was an area once owned by the family of John Fawckner.

During the Middle Ages the manor of Daventry had a succession of owners, from Countess Judith (William the Conqueror's niece and widow of Waltheof, Earl of Huntingdon) to Simon de Senlis (the builder of Northampton Castle), to Saher de Quincy, thence to the Fitzwalter family, whose ownership lasted some 200 years.

Much of the history and growth of the town can be seen through the street names, both past and present. **Abbey Street** was once called Corn Market and stands on the site of a medieval priory, whose gardens and cloisters covered the area just north of the church. Where Abbey Street and High Street meet there were once two small open spaces, called Hog Market and Horse Market, together with the old Moot Hall. The site is now occupied by **St John's Square**, named after a religious house that once stood there. In the same area **Petty Cury** was a medieval street where food was cooked and sold. The name was a corruption of the old French word 'curie' meaning 'kitchen'.

Sadly many of the old street names have gone. **Tavern Lane** (originally extending up what is now Warwick Street) was called Boudon Lane and was the site, during the 13th century, of St Mary's chapel. **New Street** was Cow Lane in the 18th century and, before that, in the 16th century, Dead Lane. **North Street** was Dogge Lane in the 16th century but is shown on earlier town plans as Baynels Lane.

Sheaf Street, where the Wheatsheaf tavern has long stood, first appeared in the 17th century. **Newlands**, which followed the line of Sheaf Street, was a name found on 16th century maps. This area was first developed in the 14th century on 'new-land' – that is, it was probably the first large urban expansion that took place in the Middle Ages, covering land formerly farmed. **Oxford Street** was once called Badby Way and, from the 13th to the 18th century, **Brook Street** was Brook End. It was a cul-de-sac ending at a stream. One of the most unusual street names is **The Pyghtles**. A pighthe or pightel in Saxon times was a 'small enclosure', a 'croft', a 'close' or a 'field'. It was commonly used in fruit-growing areas.

DEANSHANGER

The earliest known spelling of this name, Dinneshangra in AD 937, suggests a prefix with an origin from the Saxon personal name, Dynne. However, a later spelling, Daneshangr in 1202 might alternatively indicate a derivation from 'Dane', that is, a Viking settler. Still later, the spelling became Denshanger and this might suggest a third possible origin – from the Saxon word denn (a woodland pasture). It is not certain which is the true derivation, although generally in place-name study the earliest known spelling gives the most accurate evidence.

The origin of the suffix is not a matter for dispute. It comes from the Saxon hangra meaning 'slope' and most often used to mean a 'wooded slope'. Thus we probably have 'Dynne's hanging wood' or

'Dynne's wooded slope'.

To the north is the hamlet of **Puxley**. This was Pucheslei in the Domesday Book and probably derives either from Poca's leah (clearing) or from pucel – leah (goblin – clearing).

Westwards are two areas of woodland **Ashalls Copse** and **Redmoor Copse**. The former was once 'the wielle' (spring) by the aesc (ash tree); the latter was hreod – mor (reed – swamp or reedy pool).

The hamlet of **Little London** appeared only in the 18th century, probably coined as an ironic name for a settlement that was especially small.

Deanshanger is a growing village but one that keeps some of its old charm (despite being so close to Milton Keynes).

The **Dukes Head** pub was originally called the Duke of Cumberland, who was one of the sons of George III. The **Woodman's Arms**, which was built in the 1930s, recalls the fact that Deanshanger was a medieval village in the middle of Whittlebury Forest. **Dove House Farm** is probably a corruption of duffus meaning 'food house'. It was once part of the Deanshanger monastery, said to have been visited by Thomas à Becket in the 12th century.

DEENE

For the most part this is a 17th century estate village. It was built when the parkland around Deene House was landscaped. The original village now lies beneath the waters of the lake.

The village name has changed little over the centuries. In the Domesday Book it was Dene. Before that it was Den (in 1065) and after, it was Dien (in 1205). The derivation is simply from denu, the Saxon word for valley. The village stands on the Willow Brook, downstream from Corby.

On the far side of the estate is the village of **Deenethorpe**. This was simply called Torp in 1086, only later becoming Deenthorp (1246) and Dyngthorp (1538). Thorp was a word used by the Scandinavian settlers to mean, not just a village, but more specifically a 'secondary settlement' – that is, one that has been set up or colonised by a larger one nearby (in this case, Deene).

Deene Park is the historic home of the Brudenell family, the Earls of Cardigan. It was the 7th Earl who fought at the battle of Balaclava, taking part in the Charge of the Light Brigade, during the Crimean War (1854-56). It was from him that the 'cardigan' was named – he wore such a garment to keep out the Russian winter. Balaclava helmets also originated during that campaign. The weather was very cold indeed!

DENFORD

It is most likely that this was originally denu – ford, the 'ford in the valley' although some etymologists think the prefix could alternatively derive from the Saxon word derne meaning 'hidden'. In the Domesday Book the village was Deneford; this changing to Derneford and Doneford in the 13th century.

The village stands on the river Nene. It is interesting to note that the pronunciation of the name of this river changes along the stretch near Denford. Upstream (to the south) it is known as the 'Nen'; downstream (towards the Fens) it is known as the 'Neen'.

DENTON

Up to 200 years ago this village was also known as Little Doddington. Its origin is therefore linked etymologically to that of Great Doddington: from Dodda's ingtun (farmstead). The name 'Denton' evolved as a short form of 'Doddington' and came into use to distinguish this village from its bigger relation.

In the Domesday Book the name was Dodintone, this becoming Dodington in 1275 and Little Denynton in 1371. In 1483 it was recorded as Denentone. During the 18th century the two names were being used concurrently: Denton Parva and Doddington Parva. Later the 'Parva' was dropped, and later still the 'Doddington' was dropped altogether.

DESBOROUGH

From the early spellings – Dereburg (1086) and Deresburc (1166) – it is fairly clear that the suffix derives from the Saxon word burh meaning 'fortified place' or 'fort'. The prefix, however, may derive either from dis (sacred) or from deor (deer). Some historians even suggest that the prefix comes from Deor, a personal name. Thus we have 'holy fortress', 'fortified place where deer are kept' or 'Deor's fort'. In the 14th century the place was called Deseburg supra Rowell. At that time Desborough was little more than a hamlet and Rothwell was an important market town.

Buckwell Close is near the site of the old Buck Well, one of the many public wells that once supplied the town with water. It was evidently much used for washing since the word 'buck' was used in medieval times to mean 'wash'. Shakespeare, for example, mentioned a 'buckbasket' referring to a washing basket. Desborough's Buck Well became impure and was finally covered in 1900.

The old railway station was opened in 1857, shortly after which ironstone quarrying began in the town. Most of the streets in the central part of Desborough date from then to the First World War. After the quarrying company had removed the stone from the area between the railway line and the High Street, building plots and roads were laid out. These connected up with the street plan already in existence, north of Station Road, which was being developed by private enterprise (**New Street** being the first road to be completed). The Desborough Freehold Land and Building Society lasted from 1889 to 1893, in which time it had financed the building of the streets named **Victoria**, **Union**, **Havelock**, **Compton**, **King**, **Queen** and **Regent**. Havelock was a famous General at the time of the Indian Mutiny (1857), Compton is the family name of the Marquess of Northampton.

DINGLEY

Originally this was either Dynne's leah or dingle leah. Dynne would have been a Saxon personal name, whilst dingle was the Saxon word for a 'deep valley', 'hollow' or 'dell'. Leah was the word for a 'clearing' or 'glade'. In the Domesday Book of 1086 the place was called Dinglei, with various spellings appearing during the 12th and 13th centuries including Dingele, Dingeleye and Dinggele. The meaning 'clearing in a dell' would certainly suit the landscape here, for this part of Northamptonshire, east of Market Harborough, is dissected by many little valleys, producing very attractive countryside.

Dingley Hall was built in the 16th century for Sir Edward Griffin, Attorney General under Edward IV, but has been remodelled several times since then. During the 19th century it was the home of the Hungerford family; in the early 20th century it was owned by Lord Beatty, hero of the First World War.

DODFORD

This village is a long way from both Denford and Great Doddington yet it appears to have been named after the same person – a Saxon by the name of Dodda. Here we have Dodda's ford. In AD 944 it was Doddanford; in the Domesday Book (1086) it was Dodeforde; in 1166 it was Dudeford.

One suggestion that the prefix derived instead from a waterweed called 'dod', which grew along the nearby Nene meadows, has been largely discounted by etymologists.

DUDDINGTON

Situated in the north-east corner of the county this village was once set in the midst of Rockingham Forest. In the 11th century it was called Dodintone; in the 12th century Duditun and in the 13th century Dadinton. It derives from Dudda (a personal name) and ingtun (homestead or village). The Dudda in this instance is not thought to be the same person as the Dodda who gave his name to Great Doddington, Denford and Dodford.

The manor house at Duddington has been the home of the Jackson family since the 17th century.

Assart Farm was Lez Sert in the 16th century, a corruption of essart, Norman French for 'woodland clearing'. **Dales Wood** was just Dale in 1220, from dael meaning 'valley'.

DUSTON

Once a separate village this is now a north-west suburb of Northampton, with New Duston having been added to its outer edge. Called Dustone in the Domesday Book and in 1303, Doston, this could simply have been the dusty tun (farmstead): a farm located on dusty soil. However there was a Saxon word dus which meant 'heap' and a Viking word dys which meant 'grave' or 'barrow' so the name could stem from a meaning like 'farm by a burial mound'.

The **Melbourne Arms** and **Melbourne Lane** are named after Lord Melbourne, who was prime minister from 1835 to 1841. He owned much of the land in the area.

The **Hopping Hill** pub was converted in 1970 from a country house once owned by Sir Robert Fossett the circus owner.

■ EARLS BARTON

Barton is a common English place-name, coming from the Saxon words bere (barley) and tun (farm). Barley was an important crop from the Dark Ages onwards, used for animal feed and brewing. The modern word beer is from the Saxon 'beor' coming from the same root as 'bere'.

In the 12th century this particular estate was owned by the Earl of Huntingdon – the 'earl's barley farm'. From Bartone in the Domesday Book and Bertona in 1155 it became Erlesbarton in 1261.

Famous for its Saxon church tower, Earls Barton has expanded over recent years but retains much of its old charm. The manor house was once owned by the Whitworth family.

Dowthorpe End was called Barton Thorp in 1261, thorp being the Scandinavian word for a 'secondary settlement'. In the 17th century the name was Dowthorpe Townes End, this apparently being linked to a district called Dowlands. Eastwards was once a manorial estate called Widetorp, but this seems not to have survived.

The name **Berry Mount** (and **Berry Close**) is taken from the Saxon burh meaning 'fortified place'. There was once a hill fort here. **Syke Way** is a corruption of the Saxon word sic meaning a 'stream'.

The Boot pub was built in 1863 and recalls the fact that Earls Barton was once famous as a boot and shoe town. Shoes were made here, in fact, as early as the 13th century, using local leather.

EAST CARLTON

The 'East' in this name is a recent addition, introduced over the last two centuries to distinguish this village from Carlton Curlieu, not far away across the border into Leicestershire. Before it was listed in the Domesday Book as Carlintone it was called Carlatune. Later, in the 12th century, it was Carleton. The Saxon word ceorl, and the Viking word karla, were both used to indicate a 'freeman' or 'villein', that is, a man who had been released from indenture – a man who was no longer a serf. So Carlton was probably a tun (farm) inhabited by such a person.

The French chateau-style mansion was built in 1873 by the Palmer family and purchased by the Corby Steel Corporation in the 1930s. It, together with the surrounding country park is now run by the district council.

EAST FARNDON

This was simply called Ferendone in the Domesday Book, corrupted from the Saxon words fearn (fern or bracken) and dun (hill). In the 12th and 13th centuries various spellings were used, including Farnedoun, Farendone and Farndon. The 'East' was introduced in the 17th century to differentiate this settlement from West Farndon near Woodford Halse.

The **Judith Stone** is a large boulder standing in a nearby field. It is, in fact, an erratic put down by a glacier during the Ice Age, but is so named because much of the area hereabouts during the 11th century was owned by Judith, Countess of Huntingdon.

EASTON MAUDIT

There is a story that this name derives from the French word 'maldit' meaning 'cursed', and that the curse has come true. The village declined during the enclosure movement, suffered a disastrous fire (in 1738) and witnessed the fall of the Yelverton family, together with its manor house. However, the truth is more mundane. The estate was held in the 12th century by John Maled, whose family subsequently changed its name to Mauduit and Maudit.

Originally the place was just called Estun (in AD 656) and Estone (in 1086) – the est-tun (east farm), so named from its position in relation to Denton and Whiston. At one time it was called Estone juxta Boseyate (in 1305) so close is it to Bozeat.

In the late 16th century the manor was held by Sir Christopher Yelverton, the Speaker of the House of Commons who wrote the daily prayer still used in Parliament. In the 18th century the vicar was Dr Thomas Percy, friend of Oliver Goldsmith, David Garrick and Samuel Johnson.

EASTON NESTON

This double name has evolved by accident. It does not derive – as might be imagined – from the Saxon est-tun (east farm) and nes-tun (promontory farm). Instead, it has come from a single name: Estanestone (in 1086). This became Estneston by 1300. It was the tun (farmstead) belonging to a person called Eadston or Aethelstan. It was in 1610 that the first record is found of the name being (wrongly) split into two: Eston Nesson.

EASTON-ON-THE-HILL

Originally this was just the est-tun (east farm), which became Eston by the time of the Domesday Book. The 'on-the-Hill' addendum has appeared only since the 18th century. Back in the 14th century the village was known by the name Eston juxta Staunford (being next to Stamford) which distinguished it from other 'Easton' villages.

Vigo Lodge was called Vigo House in the early 19th century. It was named in honour of the British naval victory at Vigo, Spain, in 1702. **Neville Day Close** stands on the site of a reservoir constructed in the 19th century to supply water to the village. Pipes led from the reservoir to street taps. The scheme was financed by Neville Day, who also paid for the village to receive gas lighting supplied by a local gas works.

The **Exeter Arms** is named after the family of the Marquess of Exeter, which has lived at nearby Burghley House since Tudor times. The Burghley Estate owns much land in this part of north-east Northamptonshire.

One local family of historical interest was the Skynners. In 1799 the son of the Reverend John Skynner was lost at sea. He went down with the ship *La Lutine*, which was carrying a cargo of gold and silver worth £1¼ million. When the ship's bell was later recovered it was taken to the insurers, Lloyd's, where it still hangs. It is rung when bad news arrives.

ECTON

From Echentone (1086), Echeton (1164) and Ekinton (1175) we can deduce a derivation from Ecca's tun (farmstead). Ecca was possibly a local tribal leader or else an early landowner. The village today is surprisingly quiet considering its close proximity to the eastern edge of Northampton. Ecton House was once the home of Sir John Brown, First World War hero and founder of the Territorial Army.

The Worlds End Inn has a sign which reputedly was painted by William Hogarth, the 18th century artist, and given in settlement of a debt. **The Three Horseshoes** pub was built in 1757 on the site of a blacksmith's forge. This once belonged to the family ancestors of Benjamin Franklin, American writer, inventor, scientist and states-man. He was born in 1706, the son of Josiah, who had emigrated from Ecton in 1682. There are some Franklin memorials in the churchyard and the village still hosts a constant stream of American tourists.

EDGCOTE

Between the 1086 spelling, Hocecote, and the 1526 spelling, Edgecotte, many versions of this name appeared, including Ochecot, Hechcot and Hoggecote. It is thought the origin might be Hwicca's cot (cottage). There was a Saxon tribe living in the Wychwood Forest, now in Oxfordshire, called the Hwicce and this place-name could be connected with that group.

Paddle Cottage is a corruption of Padwell, a well-known spring which, in the Middle Ages, was thought to have healing qualities.

The area to the south-west of Edgcote is called **Danes Moor**. This was Danysmore in 1467, the year when the battle of Edgcote was fought during the Wars of the Roses. Tradition says that this was also the site of an earlier battle – one between Danes and Saxons in the 10th century.

ELKINGTON

This hamlet, close to the Leicestershire border, was called Eltetone in the Domesday Book. Later, in 1184, it was Eltindon and later still, in 1394, Eltyngdoun. It is thought to derive from Elta's dun (hill). Elta could have been a local tribal leader's name.

To the north is **Cot Hill**. This is named from the Saxon word cot meaning 'cottage'. Eastwards is **Honey Hill**. This was Grethonehill in the 16th century, possibly derived from 'great-hone-hill'. Hone was Saxon for a 'stone' or 'rock'. There is a large boulder here.

EVENLEY

This name derives from two Saxon words, efn (even or smooth) and leah (grove or clearing). The landscape in this area, south of Brackley, is indeed fairly flat with many small streams draining into the Great Ouse river.

In the 11th century the name was listed as Avelai and Evelaia; in the 12th century it was Euenlai.

Plowman's Furze was originally Plummer's Furze. During the 13th century the area was owned by John le Plomer, in the 14th century by his descendant Robert Plommer.

Between Evenley and Croughton is the lost village of **Astwick**, which disappeared during the Middle Ages as a result of enclosures and the extension of sheep grazing. It was Estwic in the 12th century – the 'east farm'. This was so called in relation to Croughton.

EVERDON, Great and Little

Great Everdon is usually just called Everdon, and originally there was only one village here. Little Everdon appeared later in medieval times, as a colonial or daughter village. In AD 944 it was Eferdun; in the Domesday Book (1086) Everdone. The origin was from Saxon eofor (wild boar) and dun (hill). The village stands on a slight hill, above a tributary of the upper Nene, and such a location possibly gave some safety against wild animals. Alternatively, the name might have arisen because wild boars were captured here. They were a rich source of food in those days.

Everdon is a pretty village, with many old cottages. The poet Thomas Gray, author of the *Elegy written in a Country Churchyard* often stayed here with his uncle the Reverend William Antrobus. During the following century, Arnold's Boot factory started here, set up by the great Victorian industrialist William Arnold.

Snorescombe was Snocescumb in AD 944 and Snoscoumbe in 1239, these being a corruption of the Saxon words snoc (point or projection) and cumb (valley). **Westcombe** was so called because it is west of Snorescombe.

Mantles Heath was once owned by John Mauntel – there was a Maunteleswode in 1346. **Everdon Stubbs** comes from the Saxon word stub for tree trunk. Stubbing meant 'cleared land'.

EYDON

The original version of this name was Aegas dun (hill), which is interesting, since the original of Aynho, ten miles to the south, was Aegas hoh (cliff or ridge). Either Aega was a common Saxon name or else one particular tribal leader had authority over a large area. In the Domesday Book (1086) this village was called Egedone, in 1219 Ayndona, and in 1220 Eidon.

Eydon Hall was built by Francis Annesley in the late 18th century and was owned, early in the 20th century, by Lord Brand. East of the village there was once the railway junction that led to some residential development during Victorian times. **The Manitoba estate**, of more recent date, occupies the site of allotments once owned by the Pettifer family. Medicinal herbs were once grown here. Formerly this area was called Manitoba Field. It was common for the fields located at the farthest points from a farmhouse or village to be given ironic names like Botany Bay and Gibraltar. Manitoba might be such a remote field name.

■ FARTHINGHOE

This village has been built on a grid pattern of streets, thus giving us a good example of medieval town planning. Before this redevelopment, the place was just a hamlet called Ferningeho (in the Domesday Book, 1086). The name derives from three Saxon words: fearn (fern or bracken), inga (people) and hoh (hill spur or ridge). So the original name probably meant 'the ridge of the dwellers in the bracken'. By the 12th century the spelling had become Farningho.

The **Ouse Well** is close to the source of the river Ouse. Abbey Lodge, the 15th century house next to the church of St Michael, is of great historic interest.

South-east of Farthinghoe is **Steane**, now a manor house and farm, but a thriving village in the Middle Ages. It was Stane in 1086 and

Stein in 1335 – from the Saxon stan (stone), or perhaps more accurately, staene (stony place). Nearby **Coleready Farm** was Collready in medieval times, being a corruption of col (cool) and rithig (river).

FARTHINGSTONE

Traditionally pronounced 'Farraxton', this name derives from a personal name – Faerthegn or Fardein – and the Saxon word tun meaning 'farmstead'. In the Domesday Book it was Fordinestone, this later changing to Fardeneston in the 12th century and Ferdingestone in the 13th century.

The village has a garden of remembrance called **Joymead**. This was financed, and given to Farthingstone, by Philip Agnew, High Sheriff of Northamptonshire at the beginning of the 20th century. He was the proprietor of *Punch* magazine, a JP and a much-loved local philanthropist. But tragedy struck. His son, Ewan Siegfried, was killed in the First World War and his daughter, Enid Jocelyn (Joy), died in 1921 aged only 22. Joymead was laid out in their memory.

FAWSLEY

There was once a village here – called Fealuwes Lea in AD 944 and Falesleuue in 1086 – but this disappeared with the coming of enclosures and sheep grazing. There was also once a thriving estate here – Fawsley Hall, home of the Knightley family from 1415 to the end of the 19th century – but this has fallen into a sad decay. The name comes from the Saxon words fealu (meaning 'red earth' usually referring to fallow land) and leah (clearing). In the 13th century the spelling was Falwesleye.

Nearby **Kingbrook Spinney** was once called foul brook, such was the poor condition of the local stream.

FINEDON

The suffix here does not come from dun (Saxon for hill) as might have been supposed, but from denu (Saxon for valley). The prefix derives from thinge, the Saxon word for an 'assembly'. So the site was a 'valley where meetings took place'. Various spellings are found in old documents: Tingdene in the Domesday Book, Tindena in 1167, Thingdene in 1363 and Fyndon in 1606.

The **Mulso Arms**, named from the local estate owning family, was once a farmhouse belonging to Elm Grange Farm. There is also a **Mulso Road**. **Debdale Grove** was Depdale in 1423 – a deep dale – and **Ryebury Hill** was Reberg in 1222 – a beorg (hill) where rye was grown.

FINESHADE

There was once a Norman castle here called Castle Himel – a name corrupted from the original Castro Inyel (thought to be derived from a personal name like Inyeld). Then, in the 13th century, Richard Engayne founded an Augustinian priory here. This was called Finnisheved, after a small hill called Finn's Head, or Finna's Heafod (headland). By the 14th century the name had become Fenesheved.

This part of Northamptonshire, north-east of Corby, was once covered by Rockingham Forest, and today large areas of woodland still remain. Eastwards of Fineshade is **Westhay Wood**, which was the west haeg (enclosure) in relation to Kings Cliffe. Southwards is **Lynn Wood**, which was once Lyndewode, from the Saxon lind, for 'lime tree' or 'linden'.

FLORE

Also called 'Floore' this name either comes from the Latin word 'flora' (flowers) or from the Saxon word flor (floor). Both are possible derivations. In the Domesday Book (1086) it was actually listed as Flora but this had changed to Floure by 1330.

The area has long been famous for the fertility of its soil and the botanical wealth of the local gardens. But there is also evidence that a Roman villa once stood nearby – parts of a tessellated pavement have been unearthed. Roman villas were, in fact, farmsteads. Interestingly, the Saxon 'flor' also meant 'threshing floor'.

Adams Cottage in the village, is said to have been the home of the ancestors of John Adams, the co-writer of the American Declaration of Independence who succeeded his friend George Washington as President of the USA.

To the east, **Glassthorpehill** was Clachestorp in 1086, probably a corruption of Klak's thorp (village). This was a Danish place-name, Klak being perhaps a Viking landowner.

FOTHERINGHAY

There are several theories regarding the origin of this name. One is that it derives from a personal name Froda, together with inga (people) and eg (island), giving us 'the island of Froda's tribe'. Another is that it comes from forth-here-inga-eg meaning 'the island of people following an army leader'. An alternative suggestion is that the name derives from the Saxon word fodring (foddering or enclosure used for fattening animals). There is even a possibility that the suffix comes not from eg but from heg (hay).

Sadly the early spellings do not solve this etymological puzzle. All the theories are equally likely. In 1060 it was Fodringeya; in 1075 Frodigeya, in 1168 Foderingeya and in 1212 Fotheringeia. Neither does the particular location of the village help in our investigation. Fotheringhay stands on high land slightly above the Nene meadows, so could once have been an 'island'. But it was also set in a clearing within Rockingham Forest, where animals would certainly have been grazed, and fodder crops grown.

Legend tells us that the place was called Fotheringay before the execution here of Mary Queen of Scots. Thereafter, the 'h' was added, because the village would never again be 'gay', such was its loyalty to the Catholic cause. The castle is now just a mound, but **Castle Farm** survives, once the home farm to the estate.

Walcot Lodge nearby, was Walecote in 1261. This derives from walas – cot, the 'cottage of serfs or foreigners'. Walas was the plural form of wealh and was used to mean any 'strangers' or 'underlings'. The Celts were called the Walas by the Saxons, thus giving us the modern name Wales.

■ GAYTON

Gaitone in 1162, Gainton in 1166 and Garton in the 13th century could either be from geit – tun (goat farm) or from Gaega's tun (the farmstead belonging to a tribal leader called Gaega).

This is a pleasant village south-west of Northampton, which still possesses a green where the pound once stood – an enclosure for keeping in stray animals. The junction here is called Five Ways since five roads converge. The **Eykyn Arms** pub was named after the family that has long held the manor.

South of the village is **Millmott** standing on the high ground which acts as a watershed between the Nene and Ouse rivers. The ground is often waterlogged, and willow trees flourish. There was once a mill here, and 'mott' comes from the old word for mound or hillock.

GEDDINGTON

This village boasts one of the three surviving Eleanor Crosses. These were built in 1294 by Edward I to mark the places where his wife's funeral cortège stopped overnight on its way from Harby, Nottinghamshire to Westminster Abbey. In those days the place was set in the midst of Rockingham Forest, much of which was Geddington Chase, a royal hunting forest. **Wood Street** recalls this background and, in fact, stands close to the site of the medieval royal hunting palace. It is said that stones from that palace are incorporated into the buttressed cottages along this thoroughfare.

The name of the village – Geitentone in 1086, Gattinton in 1158 and Geidinton in 1204 – derives from an old Scandinavian personal name, Geiti, and the Saxon word ingtun (homestead).

Rising Bridge was Risenbrige in the 13th century, a name corrupted from the Saxon words hris or hrisen (brushwood) and brycg (bridge). There would have been a causeway here made of branches.

Langley Quarter was Langeleghe in 1337, this being derived from the Saxon lang (long) and leah (clearing). **Great and Little Brand** were evidently places cleared by burning the original woodland, since the name comes from the Saxon word baernet meaning 'burnt'. **Sart Wood** was called Le Assart in a 1642 document, this coming from the French essart meaning a 'woodland clearing'.

The Geddington vicarage was once a preparatory school where members of the Gladstone family were educated. William Gladstone was the great Victorian prime minister.

GLAPTHORN

Also known as Glapthorne, this name has not changed since 1396. Before then it was Glaptorn (1185) and Glapetorn (1189). The suffix clearly comes from thorn ('thorn bush' or 'thorny' in Saxon times), but the prefix has three possible origins. Either it derives from glaep (sloping), or from glaeppe (a plant similar to buck-bean), or else from a personal name like Glappa. All are of Saxon origin and all are equally likely.

Provost Lodge was once Provosts Manor, and stands to the west of Glapthorn. It was once the property of a provost from the church of St Andrew at Cotterstock, endowed to house twelve chaplains during their education.

There are some fascinating old field names dotted around Glapthorn that might repay further study, including Swinner, Puckwell Hill, Casteepings, Hanging Baulk and Milking Stool.

GRAFTON REGIS

In medieval times the lords of the manor here were the Woodvilles, one of whose number, Elizabeth, married King Edward IV in 1464. This caused a sequence of events that culminated in the Wars of the Roses. Two centuries later the village returned to the pages of our history books, when Charles II made his illegitimate son Henry Fitzroy the first Duke of Grafton.

Originally the village was just called Grastone (in 1086) and Graftone (in 1166), deriving from graf (grove) and tun (farm). In the 16th century, however, the estate became a royal possession and, in 1541, Henry VIII added the appendage 'Regis' (from the Latin for 'of the king'). It is said Henry courted Anne Boleyn here.

Southwards, towards Yardley Gobion, is the **Queen's Oak**, where Elizabeth Woodville is said to have met Edward IV. It was then in the depths of Whittlewood Forest.

GRAFTON UNDERWOOD

As with the previous entry, here Grafton is a corruption of the Saxon words graf (grove) and tun (farm), so the village was originally 'farm in the woodland grove'. In the Domesday Book of 1086 it was Grastone, by 1166 it had already gained its present spelling.

Before Northamptonshire's other Grafton village was given its 'Regis' appendage there was some confusion between these two places. So during the late 14th century this one was called Grafton Underwode, in reference to the nearby Grafton Park Wood. Later it changed to Grafton juxta Craneford and Grafton juxta Keteryng, but became Grafton Underwood again in the 18th century. The village was formerly almost entirely owned by the Duke of Buccleuch, of nearby Boughton House, and accordingly the old pub (now a private residence) was called the Duke's Arms.

Grafton Park Wood was a deer park laid out by Sir Simon Simeon, lord of the manor, during the 14th century. The old boundary bank can still be seen along the western edge.

Outside the village are the remnants of a Second World War airfield where the US 8th Air Force was based. A memorial has been erected at the end of one of the old runways.

GREAT DODDINGTON

Listed simply as Dodintone in the Domesday Book and Dudinton in 1201, this name comes from Dodda's ingtun (farmstead). It is not known who Dodda was but he also gave his name to both Denton and Dodford. Denton, in fact, was once called Little Doddington, growing up as a daughter village to this settlement.

The first mention of the present name came in the 13th century, when Great Dodington was listed, thus distinguishing this place from its offspring further south. For a while during the 14th century the name Dodington Magna was also used.

Doddington Manor Farm was once the old manor house. Leading off the High Street is a thoroughfare known as **Cut-Throat Lane**, scene of a gruesome murder some years ago.

GREAT OXENDON

Little Oxendon has all but disappeared, a victim of the Black Death, medieval enclosures and the spread of sheep grazing. It lies to the north of Great Oxendon. Traces of the old lanes and cottages can just be seen in the grassy ridges of a field.

The two villages, Great and Little, were first mentioned in the 13th century, as Oxindun Maiore and Minore respectively. Before then just a single village was listed – in the Domesday Book it was Oxendene. Originally it would have been the dun (hill) where oxen grazed.

GREATWORTH

Etymologists believe that the Domesday Book version of this name, Grentevorde, is a mistake. Instead, it should have been Greuteworde. The Norman scribe, perhaps, had misheard the name. It apparently comes from the Saxon greot (gravel) and worth (enclosure). Later spellings include Gretteworth (12th century) and Greetworth (13th century).

On the western side of Greatworth, and now part of it, is **Westhorp**. This was once a separate hamlet administered by Marston St Lawrence. It was the west thorp (village). Greatworth Manor once belonged to the Pargiter family, one of whom became an ancestor of George Washington. Amy Pargiter became Laurence Washington's second wife.

Dering Cottages are named after local benefactor Lady Dering who set up an education trust and helped finance the building of the school.

A little way south of Greatworth is **Cockley Brake**, once an important railway junction for trains between Banbury, Bletchley and Northampton. All is now silent and overgrown. Cockley was cock-hlaw (cock-hill).

GREENS NORTON

Originally this was just Nortone (in 1086) or Nortune (1187), deriving from the Saxon north tun (farm). But such a common name required a distinguishing appendage. At first there was Norton-near-Toucestre (in 1325); then Norton Davy (in 1329) and finally Grenesnorton (in 1465). Henry Grene held the manor after the Davy family. The Grenes, or Greenes, remained in occupation from the early 14th century to 1500, when the last of that family, Thomas, died. He was the grandfather of Henry VIII's sixth wife, Catherine Parr.

To the north is **Field Burcote**, derived from but-cot (peasant cottage), and **Duncote**, which was Dunecote in 1227 – originally Dunna's cot. Westwards is **Caswell**, which was 'cress spring'. **Plumton** was 'plum farm' and **Kingsthorn Wood** is so named because the estate was owned by the Norman kings.

GRENDON

The story goes that, in the 14th century, the lord of the manor John de Harrington bequeathed the village to his two daughters. Accordingly the manor was split into Over Grendon and Nether Grendon (the latter at, what is now, Lower End). The two were not reunited until the Earl of Northampton acquired the estate in the 16th century. A later earl, General Hatton Compton, built Grendon

Hall in 1685. He did not live there much, however, since the family home was at nearby Castle Ashby.

In the Domesday Book of 1086 the village was listed as Grendone and in 1313 as Gryndon. The derivation was from the Saxon gren (green) and dun (hill). At the time of the Dissolution of the monasteries Henry VIII gave much of the lands hereabouts to Trinity College, Cambridge, which has owned them ever since.

GRETTON

This was simply the 'great tun' (big farm). In 1086 it was Gretone, in the early 13th century Gratton. Overlooking the Welland valley and the old county of Rutland this is a pleasant, unassuming village, once set amidst Rockingham Forest. The **Talbot** is a common pub name in these parts, being taken from a breed of hunting dog, now extinct. The **Hatton Arms** occupies a building thought to date back to the 12th century when it was part of the Carlton Manor gatehouse. According to legend it became a pub in 1672 when the licence was granted to a negro servant who had saved the life of Sir Christopher Hatton, Elizabeth I's chancellor who lived for a while at nearby Kirby Hall.

Kirby Hall stands to the south-east of Gretton, today little more than a magnificent shell. There was once a village here called Chercheberie (in 1086) and Cerkeby (in 1196). It was the by (village) near the church. The suffix is of Danish origin and it was probably Scandinavian settlers who changed the spelling and pronunciation of the soft Saxon 'chirch' to the hard Viking 'kirk'.

All around are remnants of the forest that once engulfed north-east Northamptonshire. **Thatchams Copse** was Thakholm in the early 14th century, coming from 'the thatch by the holm' (river meadow). The low-lying marshes here probably supplied reeds suitable for thatching. **Presgrave Copse** was Prestgrave in about 1400, from preost (priest) and graf (grove).

GUILSBOROUGH

Although the spelling used in the Domesday Book was Gisleburg it is thought that the suffix derives not from beorg (mound, hillock) but from burh (fortified place). The prefix is probably taken from a Saxon personal name, Golda perhaps or Gyldi. Medieval spellings of the name included Gildeburch in the 12th century and Guldesburgh in the 14th century.

Guilsborough boasts many old and interesting buildings, and has some interesting historic associations. In 1645 General Fairfax camped just to the north of the village (at Nortoft) just before the battle of Naseby. In the early 19th century the vicar here, a Reverend Sykes, was a good friend of the poet William Wordsworth, who frequently came to visit.

The **Ward Arms** was named after the lords of the manor. It once stabled the royal hunting horses.

Nortoft Lodge and Grange recall the north toft (homestead or dwelling) once used by shepherds and herdsmen, whilst tending their animals. **Lindow Spinney** is taken from lind (lime tree) and hoh (hill).

■ HACKLETON

Originally this was either Haecel's ingtun (farmstead) or haca-ingtun (the farmstead with a bolt or bar). If the former, Haecel would have been a local tribal leader or landowner. If the latter, the haca might have been used to protect the farm from marauders. In Saxon times Salcey Forest, which stretched as far as Hackleton, was the home of various wild animals including wolves and boars. The Domesday Book (1086) recorded Hochelintone. This became Haclintona by 1155 and Hakilton a century later.

The Baptist chapel here is dedicated to the memory of William Carey, the missionary who went to India in 1793 and translated the Bible into 26 Indian dialects. In his younger days he was a cobbler in Hackleton.

HADDON, East and West

The two village names we know today were first mentioned in the 13th century. Before then there was just a single place-name, listed as Edone or Hadone in 1086 and Haddun in 1185. This name derives from the Saxon haeth (heathland) and dun (hill). Both villages stand on the limestone hills once famous for sheep and cattle grazing in the centuries when the landscape was covered by heathland and open pasture.

It is likely that originally two separate villages grew up with the same name. But as confusion arose between them, distinguishing adjectives were added. Thus they became Westhaddon and Esthaddon.

East Haddon is a quiet, pretty village. The hall was built in the 19th century by the Sawbridge family, which also financed the building of the local church and various cottages.

West Haddon is the busier of the two, standing on the Northampton to Rugby road. Griggory Palmer, whose tomb will be found in the church, was born here in 1608 and was rector from 1641 to 1693.

Nearby was **Oster Hill**, a small eminence standing in a field. This was so named because legend tells us that it was the tumulus or burial mound of Ostorius Scapula, Roman governor under Emperor Claudius. **Hungerwell Barn** was once hangra wielle – 'hanging spring', that is, a spring flowing down a steep slope.

HANNINGTON

The 13th century church stands on the site of an old monastery belonging to the Gilbertine order of monks. Thomas à Becket is said to have taken refuge here after his escape from Northampton Castle, whilst evading Henry II's troops.

Hannington Grange, to the north-east of the village, towards Kettering, was once the outlying farm belonging to the monastery. The village name itself was Hanitone in the Domesday Book and Haninton in 1195. It derived from Hana's ingtun (farmstead). Hana might have been a local Saxon leader.

HARDINGSTONE

Now almost a southern suburb of Northampton, Hardingstone was once a small village famous only for having a heavily restored example of an Eleanor Cross. The original was erected in 1294 to commemorate the journey Edward I's dead wife had made four years earlier from Nottinghamshire to London. The funeral procession stopped overnight at nearby De La Pre Abbey, which belonged to one of the few Cluniac orders of nuns in England.

In the Domesday Book (1086) the village was listed both as Hardingestorp and Hardingestone. Etymologists suggest, however, that the suffix derives neither from thorp (village) nor tun (farmstead). They say, instead, it comes from thorn, the Saxon word for 'thorn bush' or 'thorny'. Perhaps closer to the original spelling was Hardighestorn, in 1145. The prefix comes from a personal name, Hearding.

There was an old paper mill at Rush Mills, and here the paper used for the first penny black stamp was made. The village pond, known as **The Basin**, was once thought to be bottomless.

The name **Rouse Corner** has an interesting history. In 1930 a certain Alfred Rouse faked his own death by setting fire to his car with an unconscious hitchhiker inside, so the charred body would be thought his. But he was captured and hanged for the murder of the hitchhiker. The identity of that hitchhiker, however, was never discovered.

HARDWICK

The Domesday Book version of this name was Herdewiche but an earlier spelling (Heordewican, in 1067) was more closely linked to the Saxon original. Heorde was Saxon for 'flock' and wic meant 'farm'. So the early spelling was the dative plural of these and meant 'at the sheep farms'. By 1220 the name had become Herdwyk.

The present manor house is 17th century, but the first to be built here was used by the Knights Templar and later by the Knights Hospitallers of St John of Jerusalem.

HARGRAVE

This village stands close to the Bedfordshire and Cambridgeshire borders, a fact that might have led to its name. The Saxon word har meant 'boundary' and could have given us the present prefix. Alternatively the first element could be derived from here (Saxon for 'army') or hara (Saxon for 'hare'). Given that the suffix is a corruption of graf (grove) we have the possible meanings 'boundary grove', 'army grove' or 'grove where hares are found'. In Saxon times hares were numerous and provided an important source of food. Rabbits were introduced into England by the Normans.

Two spellings for this name were used in the Domesday Book, Haregrave and Heregrave. By the 12th century it had become Haragrava. So all these possible origins could be true.

HARLESTONE

The old theory that this name derives from the Saxon words haeth (heathland) and stan (stone) is not supported by etymological evidence. The landscape hereabouts is certainly heathy and stony but the origin of the name is, in fact, Herewulf's tun (farmstead). In 1086 it was Herolvestone, in 1169 Herleston and in 1231 Herlestune.

During the Middle Ages two Harlestone villages developed, Upper and Lower, the former being to the south (beyond the old landscaped parkland as we know today). Mention of **Harlestone Heath**, to the south-east towards Northampton, first appeared in 1287 as Herlestonheth. This later became the site of a racecourse.

Nearby **Fleetland Farm** was Fflitlond in Saxon times, from flitenlond (land in dispute). **Sowditch Thicket** was the 'south ditch' and **Dudman's Plantation** takes its name from a Saxon owner Dudeman.

HARPOLE

The earliest spellings – Horpol and Horepol in the 11th century – indicate a derivation from horh (dirty or muddy) and pol (both the Celtic and Saxon word for 'pool' or 'lake'). Whether this referred to the village pond, or to a river mere in the nearby Nene meadows, is not known. In 1258 the name was recorded as Harepol and in 1557 as Happall.

Flitnell Barn was Fletynhyll in the Middle Ages, a name derived from fliten-hyll (a hill subject to a dispute). **Blackwell's Farm** is named after the Blackwell family, which owned the land in the 18th century.

HARRINGTON

Interestingly, the spelling used in 1184, Hederingeton, was closer to the origin than the Domesday Book spelling, Arintone. In early Saxon times the place was probably Haethhere's ingtun (farmstead). Haeth-here could have been Saxon for 'heath-army' but, in this instance, such would not have made sense either historically or geographically. In 1526 the name was Hathrington.

A Tudor manor house once stood to the west of the village, a site now occupied by a pasture field. In more recent times the estate was owned by the Naylor family and, after 1913, by the Desborough Co-operative Society, which sold the lands off in 1927. The church of St Peter and St Paul was originally dedicated to St Botolph.

The **Tollemache Arms** was named after the 19th century rector Hugh Tollemache, who purchased the pub in order to close it every Sunday. Only in this way could he persuade the locals to attend his services. He installed a landlord and remained rector until 1890, having served his congregation for 58 years.

The hamlet **Thorpe Underwood**, nearby, was Torp in 1206 and Torp Underwode in 1255. It was the 'secondary settlement' near a forest. To the east is **Hospital Farm**, once owned by the Jesus Hospital, Rothwell, and further south **Nunnery Farm**, once owned by Rothwell's old nunnery.

The name **Loatland**, as used for a wood and a farm, was Louteland in the 13th century. This probably derived from the Scandinavian words laut (hollow, small valley) and lundr (grove, copse).

Newbottle Bridge is so named because lands here were once owned by William de Newebotl (a village near Charlton). **Wharf Lodge** is probably a corruption of the old Norse word vartha meaning a 'cairn' or 'heap of stones'.

71

HARRINGWORTH

Now famous for its splendid Victorian viaduct, which marches across the Welland valley into the old county of Rutland, Harringworth was an important settlement in medieval times. Near the old manor house is the **White Swan**, said to be one of the oldest pubs in the county, having served beer since Tudor times.

In 1060 the village was Haringwrth, in 1086 Haringeworde and in 1323 Harryngworth. It derives from Hering's worth (enclosure). **Turtle Bridge** was Thurkelbregge in the Middle Ages. The lands here were owned by Ralph Turcle.

HARROWDEN, Great and Little

These separate village names first appeared in documents of the 15th and 16th centuries, where they were listed as Maior and Parva (from the Latin forms of 'great' and 'little', otherwise 'major' and 'minor'). Before then only a single name was recorded: Hargindone (1086), Harhgeduna (1155), Harudon (1280) and Hareudon (14th century). The place was evidently a site used for heathen worship, since the derivation is from hearg (pagan shrine) and dun (hill).

Little Harrowden, now the larger of the two, grew as a small industrial village in the 19th century. **Furnace Lane** once possessed no less than six blast furnaces operated by the Glendon Iron Ore Company. The **Ten O'Clock** is the only pub in England with that name.

Great Harrowden Hall was first built in the 16th century for the Vaux family, one of whom was the poet Thomas Vaux. It was later re-modelled and owned by Lord Rockingham, prime minister during the 18th century.

HARTWELL

Unusually for a place-name the origin here is exactly as it appears: 'hart's well'. Heorot, or heort, was Saxon for 'hart' or 'male deer' and wielle meant 'well' or 'spring'. In the Domesday Book (1086) the name was Hertewelle, in 1148 Hertwella and in 1675 Harwell.

Wild deer were common in the forests of Saxon England and provided the peasants with much-needed meat supplies, and the aristocrats with much-enjoyed sport in the form of hunting.

This area was especially well-wooded, many of the trees surviving to this day. **Rowley Wood** is probably a corruption of the Saxon ruh (rough) and leah (glade, forest clearing).

Salcey Forest, immediately to the east of Hartwell, is named from an old Norman French word salceie meaning 'willow'. Incidentally, the root word for this, the Latin salicetum, also gave us our modern word sallow, a type of willow tree, and the botanical word salix.

To the south is **Chapel Farm**. Hartwell was once a chapelry of Roade.

HASELBECH

The prefix here certainly seems to come from haesel, the Saxon word for 'hazel tree', but the suffix does not come from any Saxon word for 'beech tree'. Instead it is thought to derive from the Saxon word beche or bache. Curiously this meant both 'hill' and 'valley'. It is believed the word was originally used for a valley between two hills, and the meaning subsequently became confused. The present spelling first appeared as early as the 13th century. Before then, in the 1086 Domesday Book it was Esbece.

From the Treshams the estate passed to the Wykes family in the 17th century. In the 19th century the village grew with buildings financed by Selina, Viscountess Milton, a much loved estate owner.

HELLIDON

Close to the Warwickshire border this village stands not only on the Jurassic Way, a prehistoric trackway running along the limestone hills from the Severn to the Humber, but also on an old Salt Way, used for the transport of salt from Cheshire to south-east England. The old village was not short of water: there were once 28 wells here, in addition to three streams that ran down to the river Leam. **Stockwell Lane** evidently takes its name from a well, or spring, that was used for watering cattle.

The derivation of the name Hellidon has created problems for etymologists. Whilst the suffix is clearly from dun (hill), the prefix has no less than five possible origins. It could be from one of the following Saxon words: Haegla (a personal name), haelig (slippery), halig (holy), haeg (enclosure) or hals (steep). In the 12th century the name was recorded as Elliden and Helidon, in the 13th century as Heylidere and Haliden.

Attlefield Barn is a corruption of Aetla's feld (open space, enclosure).

HELMDON

Here the suffix derives not from dun (hill) as might have been expected, but from denu (valley). The village stands on an upper tributary of the river Tove. The prefix is from a Saxon personal name, Helma. In the Domesday Book it was Elmedene, in 1162 Holmeden and in 1166 Helmesden.

The village grew quickly during the 19th century as a result of industrial expansion. The quarries around here supplied limestone for building large parts of Brackley and Towcester, and a rail junction linked Helmdon with Birmingham, Oxford and Northampton.

Now almost joined to the village at its southern end is **Falcutt**. This was Faucot in 1220 and Falcote in 1268. Fag was a Saxon word for 'variegated' and usually referred to a mixture of building materials. Cote or cot was a 'cottage' – obviously built with a jumble of different stones.

Nearby **Stockings Farm** could be corrupted from the Saxon stocc for a 'stump' or 'trunk'. West of Helmdon is **Grange Farm** which was Grounds Farm in 1823. 'Grounds' was a name often used for an outlying grazing area: a pasture field away from a village.

North-eastwards towards Wappenham is **Astwell**, which was Estwelle in 1086 – the east wielle (spring). This is the site of a castle and 16th century fortified manor house.

HEMINGTON

In the north-east corner of the county, this village has declined in size over the centuries. It was Heminton in the Domesday Book and Hamintone a century later in 1184. In 1219 it was Hemmington. Originally it would have been Hemma's ingtun (farmstead).

Beaulieu Hall comes from the Norman French name beau-lieu meaning 'beautiful place'. Westwards from here is **Ellands Farm**. In the 13th century this was called Le Heyland, being a corruption of the Saxon words heg (hay) or haeg (enclosure) and land (land or territory).

HEYFORD, Nether and Upper

In early medieval times just one settlement stood here, called Haiford (in 1086) and Heiford (in 1178). These derived from several possibilities: 'ford by the enclosure' (from Saxon haeg); 'ford by the hedge' (from Saxon hege) or 'ford over which hay was carried' (from Saxon heg). As the two separate villages developed, however, distinguishing adjectives had to be employed. So, in the early 13th century, there was Superiore and Inferiore, and in the late 13th century there was Nether and Over. For a short while Nether Heyford was even called Great Heyford.

The **Forester's Arms** recalls that this area was once densely wooded, the Nene meadows offering fertile soils for willows, ash and alder trees. The nearby school was originally called the Bliss Charity School, being endowed by the wine merchant William Bliss in 1674. The present site was developed in the 1880s.

Furnace Lane is named after the three blast furnaces which operated here until 1891. At that time Nether Heyford was an industrial village with iron works producing steel and clay works producing bricks and tiles.

The manor house was the home of Francis Morgan in the 16th century. He was the judge who sentenced Lady Jane Grey to death in 1553.

The **Horestone Brook**, which flows through Nether Heyford to the Nene, takes its name from a boundary or marker stone. This indicated the point where the hundreds of Towcester, Fawsley and Nobottle met.

HIGHAM FERRERS

This was literally the 'high ham', a farmstead or village that stood high above the Nene meadows. In the 12th century the estate was held by the Comes de Ferariis, whose descendant was William de Ferrers, the first Earl of Derby. This family name was tacked on to the name of the village. So from Hecham (in 1086) and Hekham (in 1247) it became Higham Ferys (in 1517).

Since the time of the Wars of the Roses the manor of Higham Ferrers has belonged to the Duchy of Lancaster, and has served as a local administrative centre for Crown lands in the region. Many of the names in and around the town recall this ownership: **Duchy Farm,Lancaster Farm**, **Lancaster Street**, **Duchy Close** and so on. Even modern roads imply royalty – **Elizabeth Way, Charles Close, Anne Close, Andrew Close, Edward Close**.

The town's famous son, Henry Chichele (1360-1443), is remembered in **Chichele Close**. He was born here, attended the old grammar school and later, having become Archbishop of Canterbury, founded both Chichele College and the Bedehouse Hospital. He also re-endowed his old school. The old college, in **College Street**, survives in remnants and as an attractive garden situated behind a medieval wall. In Tudor times the lands formerly belonging to Chichele College were taken over by the Dacres family and later by the Earls Fitzwilliam, the Marquess of Rockingham line.

Some hints of medieval Higham have survived here and there. The site of the castle is now a park and recreation ground, the Bede House and church still provide a quiet corner. **Saffron Road** and the old **Saffron Moat** are so named because saffron was grown here in the Middle Ages, a plant used for flavourings and dyes. **Windmill Banks** was the site of an old windmill and **Vine Hill Drive and Close** are situated where Vine Hill Farm once stood.

Sadly some street names have changed over the years. Nene Road was once called Rogues Lane, Cemetery Lane was Parkers Lane and Chichele Close, Town Yard. Other street names have a more recent origin. **Midland Road** recalls the Midland Railway which opened its

76

line from Leicester to Hitchin (and later on to London's St Pancras) in 1857. At first a station was sited only at Irchester, to serve Higham, but in 1893 a single track extension was laid from Wellingborough to Rushden, via the eastern edge of Higham.

John White Close was built in 1951 by the John White Memorial Trust to provide homes for elderly residents. Higham Ferrers, and its neighbour Rushden, have long been centres for the boot and shoe industry.

HINTON

This name does not come from hea-tun (high farm) as some people have suggested, but from higna-tun, Saxon for 'monks' farm'. The word higna, or hiwan, was used in early medieval times to mean a monastic group – either a family dedicated to a religious life, or a community of devout men and women. The early spellings of this name include Hintone (1086), Hynton (1279) and Hyneton (1199). In the 14th century it was called Hynton by Woodford, to distinguish this village from the Hinton near Brackley (which is now Hinton-in-the-Hedges). Woodford Halse is adjacent to Hinton but the two places have preserved their identities.

To the south-west is **West Farndon**. This was just Farendun in the 12th century, derived from the Saxon fearn-dun (ferny or bracken – hill). The adjective appeared later to distinguish the place from East Farndon near Market Harborough.

Further south-west still is **Warden Grange**. This was once a farm belonging to the monks of Warden Abbey in Bedfordshire.

HINTON-IN-THE-HEDGES

As with other Hinton place-names (see above) this probably derives from the Saxon higna-tun (monks' farm). It was Hintone in the Domesday Book and Hynton juxta Brakele (Brackley) in 1285. The present name dates from the 18th century when the open fields hereabouts were enclosed for sheep grazing, the new hedges being made of hawthorn.

The **Crewe Arms** pub is named after the Crewe family, which lived for many years at Steane. Thomas Crewe was MP for Brackley in the late 17th century. The Crewes also founded the almshouses here.

HOLCOT

This was listed as Holecote in the Domesday Book, Holokote in 1250 and Hollecot in 1368. The name derives from the Saxon words holh (hollow) and cot – 'the cottage in the hollow'.

Holcot is a pleasant, quiet village set in the undulating countryside north of Northampton. It has been the long-time home of the New Guinea Mission. It still has its old town well and restored fish ponds, together with the site of a medieval wash pit.

HOLDENBY

Originally the name was Halfdan's by. Halfdan, or Haldan, was a common Viking name and by was the Scandinavian word for 'farmstead' or 'settlement'. The earliest spellings (Aldenesbi in 1086 and Aldenebi in 1184) have led some people to suggest an alternative derivation – from ald for 'alder tree' – but this is not supported by etymological study. Later spellings included Haldaneby (in 1247) and Holmby (in 1568), the latter being similar to the present pronunciation.

In the grounds of Holdenby House is the **Kings Walk** named from Charles I who used to walk in the gardens here whilst held prisoner in 1647. The estate was once owned by Sir Christopher Hatton, Queen Elizabeth I's chancellor.

Delf and **Twigden** are names of two spinneys nearby, the former comes from the Saxon word for a 'mine' or 'quarry', the latter from George Twigden one-time owner.

HOLLOWELL

The derivation of this name is the same as it sounds – the 'hollow well'. The prefix comes from the Saxon holh meaning 'hollow' or 'depression' and the suffix originates from the Saxon waella or wielle meaning 'well' or 'spring'. So the settlement was sited by a 'spring in a hollow' or by a 'deep well'. The name was Holewelle in 1086, Hollewelle in 1166 and Hollywell in 1595.

There are numerous springs and streams in this part of the county, which accounts for the siting nearby in recent years of two reservoirs.

HORTON

Situated between Salcey Forest and Yardley Chase, this village must have been isolated in Saxon times, surrounded as it was by dense woodland. The soils are heavy too in this part of Northamptonshire, so it may be no surprise that this place name comes from horh-tun meaning 'muddy farm'. Interestingly, the present spelling was used in the Domesday Book, although, in 1301, it was listed as Hurton.

Cheyney Farm, to the south and close to the Buckinghamshire border, was named after the family of Ralph de Cheney, who owned lands in Salcey Forest.

Horton was the birthplace of Charles Montagu, who established the Bank of England in 1694 and became the first Earl of Halifax. In earlier times, the village was also the home of the Parr family, one of whom, Catherine, became the sixth and last wife of Henry VIII.

HOUGHTON, Great and Little

The modern pronunciation of this name must have come directly from the spelling found in the Domesday Book – Hohton. This was unchanged from the Saxon derivation, which was hoh (spur of land or ridge) and tun (farmstead). Both Great and Little Houghton stand high above the Nene valley and must have occupied significant defensive sites when first built. Later spellings include Hoctona (1131), Houtona (1197) and Houctone (1233). The separate villages we know today grew up in medieval times as mother and daughter villages, arising when the original settlement (probably Great Houghton) set up a colonial settlement nearby to house its overspill population.

North of Little Houghton is the ancient site of **Clifford Hill**, over-looking an Iron Age crossing point of the Nene. The name derives from 'ford by the river cliff'.

79

Only three families have held the Little Houghton estate since Norman times, the de Houghtons, the Wards and the Smyths.

Great Houghton was once on a railway line, linking Northampton with Bedford, and many signs of that Victorian era still survive.

John Clare, the peasant poet, used to walk the countryside around these Houghton villages during his years at Northampton Asylum.

■ IRCHESTER

The 'chester' in this name is a corruption of the Saxon ceaster meaning 'Roman camp' or 'old fort'. Like 'cester' it is a common suffix in English place-names and usually denotes the site of a town developed by the Romans. Winchester, Colchester, Leicester, Bicester and others are all examples of Roman settlements. Here at Irchester Romano-British remains have been discovered but the settlement that existed here in the 3rd and 4th centuries AD is not thought to have been large.

The prefix might come from the Saxon iren (iron) but is more likely to derive from Ira, a Saxon personal name, judging from the etymological evidence. In AD 973 the place was called Yranceoster, in the Domesday Book (1086) it was Irencestre and in 1261 Irnecestre.

This village may not have been an 'iron fortress' but it has certainly been the site of iron-ore extraction over the centuries. The last of the quarries closed in 1941. It was called **Wembley Pit** owing to its tremendous size, thought to have been commensurate with Wembley Stadium. The disfigured ironstone workings have now been transformed into the Irchester Country Park.

The church of St Katherine has a weather vane resembling a spiked wheel, recalling the instrument on which the saint was martyred in AD 307 (hence the name of the firework 'Catherine Wheel' as used today).

Nearby **Knuston Hall**, a building of mixed styles from Jacobean to Victorian, is named from an old settlement here, called Cnutestone in 1086 and Cnoteston in 1220. This would have been Cnut's tun (farmstead) originally. At the end of the 19th century the hall belonged to Robert Arkwright, grandson of Richard, the inventor of the 'Spinning Jenny'. The **Arkwright Estate** in Irchester was named after him. It also stands on the site of a medieval manor house.

IRTHLINGBOROUGH

The earliest known spelling for this name is Yrtlingaburg, which was recorded in an AD 780 document. From this, etymologists have deduced that, whilst the suffix clearly comes from burh (fortified place or fort), the prefix could have one of two possible derivations. Either it comes from a Saxon personal name – Urtila or Yrtla – or from the Saxon word wyrt meaning 'root'. Of the two the former is the more likely. By the time of the Domesday Book the name was Erdinburne; in 1125 it was Hirtlingaburch.

Nearby **Ditchford Mill** was Dichesford in 1235 and Dickford Mulnes in 1282. It was a mill built near a ford by a dic (ditch).

Most of Irthlingborough has grown up since the 19th century, when industrialisation and the coming of the railways brought prosperity to the area.

Station Road once ran continuously from the town centre to the Nene meadows, where stood the railway station. This served the Northampton to Peterborough line, which opened in 1845. At the bottom end was the Railway Arms which was demolished in 1986. It was formerly called St Peters Arms. **New Street** was built at the beginning of the 20th century to connect Station Road with Lilley Terrace. There had not formerly been a road or path there. The **Hayway Estate** was built on the site of Hay Lane, once merely a farm track.

Two modern street names that recall Irthlingborough's earlier history are **John Pyel Road** and **College Street**. John Pyel was a merchant who became Lord Mayor of London in 1373. Having family connections with the area, he founded a college here for a dean, four clerks and five canons. This college stood close to the church. Today, only the old cellars remain to remind us of the medieval building that once graced the town centre.

Another name which conjures up the past is not a street name but

81

a field name. This is **Coneygears**, near the bottom end of Station Road, and is a corruption of coney garth – a 'rabbit enclosure'. Until the 16th century there was also a church here, All Saints, but this name has gone forever.

ISHAM

At one time this parish was divided into two, Isham Superior and Isham Inferior, situated on the higher and lower ground respectively. But early records make no mention of this division. They list just one name: Ysham in 1060, Hisham in 1086, Isam in 1235. Interestingly, the present name pre-dates all these spellings, first appearing as early as AD 974. The origin is simply the Ise-ham, the village on the river Ise.

The Ise itself has a long history as a name. It was called the Ysan in the 10th century, a corruption of the Saxon word use or ouse meaning 'water'. This in turn was connected to the Celtic word ud and, earlier still, the ancient Sanskrit word udan.

In the garden of **Manor Farm** is the dovecote that once formed part of the Elizabethan manor house, which was demolished in 1824.

ISLIP

Across the Nene from Thrapston, this village has retained its quiet unspoilt character. In the 10th century it was called Hyslepe, in the Domesday Book Islep and in 1175 Islepe. The suffix derives from the Saxon slaepe meaning 'slippery place'. The prefix has two possible origins however. Either it comes from the Saxon word hyse meaning 'young man' or 'warrior', or else from the Saxon word ise. If the latter, confusion might have arisen between the river Ise, some distance away, and words like yse and ouse which simply meant 'water'.

Drayton House is a long way off, near Lowick, but two other manor houses once stood much closer. These were the Kings Manor, which belonged to the royal estates at Brigstock, and Montagu Manor. The latter was owned in medieval times by the Bishops of Coutance. After its demolition, some of the stonework was incorporated into the old cottages in the High Street.

■ KELMARSH

This name has various possible origins, each of which is likely etymologically. The early spellings include Cailmare and Keilmerse in the 11th century, Chailesmers in the 12th century and Keylemerch in the 14th century. The prefix could derive either from a Saxon personal name, Caegla, or else from a Scandinavian word keill or keila meaning a 'rent', 'cleft' or 'fissure'. The suffix could originate from marr or mere (Saxon words for 'marsh' and 'lake') or else from mearc (Saxon for 'boundary' and connected with our modern words 'march' and 'margin').

Nearby **Shipley Wood** was Shyplegh in 1257, a name coming from the Saxon sceap-leah ('sheep-clearing').

Kelmarsh Hall, in whose grounds a herd of rare British white cattle is still grazed, was once the home of Lord Bateman. It was built to the design of the famous architect James Gibbs in 1728 for the antiquarian William Hanbury.

KETTERING

Names ending with 'ing' usually derive from the early Saxon word inga or ingas meaning 'the people of' or 'tribe'. This is no exception, and we can see this root in the spellings used in the 10th century – Cytringan, Kyteringas and Keteiringan.

The prefix in this name, however, is more difficult to translate. Some say it comes from a tribal leader's name – Cuthfrith or Cutfrith – but other possibilities have been suggested. One is that it is from cetel, the Saxon word for a 'narrow valley'; another is that it derives from cyta, the Saxon for a kite. Kites were common birds of prey in early medieval times. In the Domesday Book (1086) the spelling was Cateringe and in 1557 Ketteryng.

Wicksteed Park, on the southern edge of Kettering, was given to the town by Charles Wicksteed. He became a wealthy Victorian industrialist, having designed and manufactured a revolutionary steam plough. Much of his wealth he donated to good causes. Here his ambition was to create a pleasure park for the enjoyment of Kettering residents and especially for their children.

The town grew mostly during the 19th century with the expansion of the boot and shoe industry and the coming of the railway line. Many of the street names reflect the history of this growth and the various people who have put Kettering on the map.

In medieval times this area was covered by forests and farmlands, cottages and farms. The village of Kettering came under the jurisdiction of the Huxloe Hundred, which also incorporated places as far apart as Barnwell, Barton Seagrave, Islip and Lowick. The central meeting place was near Drayton, in a field still called Huxlow, a name incidentally deriving from Hoc's hlaw (barrow or hill). Kettering's **Huxloe Place**, off the High Street, recalls this old Hundred.

On the other side of the High Street is **Wadcroft**. In Saxon times this was probably the croft (enclosed land or smallholding) where wad (woad) was grown. This was a plant used in the making of dyes, especially those requiring a blue colouring.

To the north of here is **Northall Street**. This was Northolde in 1577, being a corruption of north-wold. Wold was Saxon for 'weald' or 'woodland'. The trees growing in this area separated the enclosed fields surrounding Kettering village from the more open fields and common pastures beyond the parish boundaries.

Another name that recalls medieval farming is **Headlands**. This comes from the old word for that part of a field left unploughed. At the end of each strip and furlong the horse-ploughs would turn round, leaving behind heaps or heads, running at right angles to the furrows.

Further away is **Links Lodge**. This name probably derives from the Saxon word hlinc meaning a 'bank', 'slope' or 'ridge'. It was most often used to indicate an embankment between two arable strips or furrows.

Much of the land on which Kettering has been built formed part of two manorial estates, those belonging to the Rockingham family and the Dukes of Buccleuch (who own nearby Boughton House). Not surprisingly therefore, many of the modern street names reflect these aristocratic connections: **Rockingham Road**, **Duke Street**, **Buccleuch Street**, **Dalkeith Place**, **Montagu Street** and so on. Dalkeith, incidentally, is the honorary title of the eldest son of the Duke of Buccleuch, whose family name is Montagu.

One area not owned by the Rockingham and Buccleuch estates was north of Northall. This was owned by John Robinson, the philanthropist who worked so hard to improve the conditions of the poor. His farmhouse stood on the south side of Northall and his farmland, totalling 110 acres, lay on the north side. The area was built over in the mid 19th century, such roads as **Upper Field Street** and **Field Street Avenue** now recalling the old landscape.

In many towns in England, street names often recall the traders and craftsmen who once lived and worked in their own distinct quarters or districts. Kettering is typical of this. **Gold Street**, **Silver Street**, **Tanners Lane** and **Sheep Street** are such examples and are self-explanatory. **Horse Market**, once called Hog Leys because pigs were fed there, became a general site for the buying and selling of animals. **Belfry Lane**, off Wadcroft, was formerly Bell Foundry Lane and named after Thomas Eayre's Bell Foundry.

Sadly many old street names have disappeared. **Market Street** was once called Parkstile Lane and **Walker Lane** was Pudding Bag Lane because it was a cul-de-sac. At the bottom of Gold Street was Bakehouse Hill, named after an old bakery. Gold Street itself was Paul Street in the 18th century after two surgeons, father and son, Hugh and Matthew Paul. **Meadow Road** has been called Mill Lane and Gas Street, but before the 19th century was known as Goose Pasture Lane. Geese were once fed here prior to being sold at market. **Lower Street** and its continuation into Rothwell Road was once Staunch Lane. This recalls the days when Kettering was famous for supplying the medical profession with stones which when ground into a powder helped to stop bleeding.

Streets named after famous residents of the past are also common in Kettering. Sir Alfred East, the 19th century artist whose name adorns the Art Gallery, is also remembered in **Alfred Street** and his contemporary Thomas Cooper Gotch, another artist, is recalled in **Gotch Road** and **Gotch Close**. Thomas's brother, John Alfred Gotch, was the renowned architect responsible for many of Kettering's famous buildings.

Victorian Kettering was the centre of 19th century religious non-conformity and the missionary movement, and this has been preserved in many of the names. William Carey was the first of the great and good men associated with the town. He was born in 1761 at Paulerspury and spent much of his young life in Kettering before leaving for India as a missionary in 1793. The **Carey Mission House** and **Carey Street** are named after him. Andrew Fuller helped Carey found the Baptist Missionary Society and he is remembered in the **Fuller Church** and **Fuller Street**. In 1803 William Knibb was born in Market Street and he grew up to continue the missionary work of Carey: he is commemorated by the **Knibb Centre** and **Knibb Street**. The **Toller Chapel** and **Toller Place** are named after two ministers, father and son, who preached in Kettering for a total of 100 years. The chapel was built in 1723 for those independents who since 1662 had been worshipping in secret.

Sawyer's Almshouses were named after another kindly man – Edmund Sawyer. He lived in the 17th century and financed the building of these cottages to house the poor and needy. Of later date is **Lindsay Street**, built in the second half of the 19th century. At that time Canon Henry Lindsay was rector (from 1861 to 1892) and he worked tirelessly for the sick. He also set up the Church Institute.

Dryland Street was once called Workhouse Lane owing to the location of the old poorhouse there. The road was renamed at the beginning of the 20th century soon after the sudden death of John Winter Dryland. The Dryland Memorial was erected in Sheep Street in 1906. J.W. Dryland settled in Kettering in 1857, setting up his doctor's practice at the corner of High Street and what was then Workhouse Lane. Soon he became a much loved and respected pillar of the local establishment. He was adviser to the workhouse (later the Poor Law Institute), medical officer to the council and chief medical adviser to the Midland Railway, the post office and fire brigade. It was largely due to his efforts that the Isolation Hospital was built in 1897. This became Rockingham Road Hospital, a site now occupied by the Paddocks housing estate. Dr Dryland's son, Leslie Winter Dryland, continued his father's good work, continuing the doctor's practice until 1942.

Of the numerous pubs in Kettering, a few have interesting names. The **Buccleuch**, of course, is named after the Duke who lives at nearby Boughton House. The **Cordwainer** and **Leathercraftsman** both recall Kettering's history as a centre for the boot and shoe industry. Perhaps the most curious of all pub names is the **Mikado Pheasant**. This is named after the game bird introduced into England in 1906 by the explorer and ornithologist Walter Goodfellow. The bird was a native of Taiwan (once called Formosa) and named after the Emperor of Japan. Goodfellow was a native of Kettering.

KILSBY

From Kildesbig in 1043, this became Chidesbi in the Domesday Book of 1086, and Childebia in 1225. The suffix is evidently from by (Scandinavian for 'farmstead') but the prefix could either be a corruption of a tribal leader's name, Kild or Childa, or else be derived from cild, Saxon for 'young man' or 'child'. If the latter were true, then the farm might have been occupied by a landowner's son. When the sons of Saxon farmers reached maturity they would often leave home and set up their own farms.

In the Middle Ages Kilsby was an important centre for sheep trading. It stood where two drove roads crossed: Main Road followed the route of the Cambridge to Coventry drove (via Welford) and Rugby Road followed the Northampton-Coventry route (via Long Buckby). **Devon Ox Road** is where the Devon Ox Inn stood before being demolished in the 1930s.

The Kilsby railway tunnel was finished in 1838, built under the direction of George Stephenson, son of Robert, the railway pioneer. The George Hotel was rebuilt at that time as well, using brick to replace the original stone structure.

Manor Road was once called Church Walk and **Middle Street** was called Cottage Close. **Smarts Estate** was built in the late 1940s and named after a local churchwarden and benefactor who died in 1942. **Essen Lane** was named after the Essen family, whose farmhouse is now called The Haven (with Sundial Cottage being the old farm-workers' cottage). Joseph Essen, who died in 1829, left a widow and two daughters. These three women later ran the village butchery and one of the daughters also set up a small private school.

KINGS CLIFFE

The name was simply Clive in the Domesday Book, later becoming Clyve and Cleve. This derived from the Saxon word clif meaning 'steep slope' (hence our modern word cliff). But when the estate soon passed to the ownership of the Norman kings, the present addendum was added. In 1305 the name Kyngesclive was recorded.

The village stands on a slope overlooking the Willow Brook, in a part of Northamptonshire that has always been sparsely populated. In

Saxon times Rockingham Forest spread this far and still many woodlands survive. **Buxton Wood** was Buckston Sale in the Middle Ages, named after Roger Bucstan. Sale was an old dialect word for a division of forest land. To its south is **Westhay Wood**. This was Westheye in the 13th century, from west haeg (enclosure). To the east of here is **Law's Lawn**, once owned by the Law family and originally called a laund, a Saxon word meaning an 'open space within a woodland'.

Other interesting names around King's Cliffe include **Calvey Wood**, called Caleweheye in the 13th century from the Saxon calu (bare or bald) and haeg (enclosure), and **Stockings**, originally called Stocking Sale from stocc (trunk or stump) and sale (a division of woodland). **Setehill** was Setehul in the 14th century, from the Saxon words set (camp or entrenchment) and hyll (hill).

Kings Cliffe is an old and interesting village, once known as the 'wooden spoon village' because of the wooden ware it used to make. It is also famous as the birthplace in 1686 of William Law, theologian, writer and philosopher. His library survives and also the almshouses he helped to set up. The **Cornforth Homes** almshouses were endowed by Mrs Cornforth in 1891.

The **Old Warren** occupies the site of the Norman castle used by King John. He also owned a manor house and hunting lodge nearby. Later in the Middle Ages Kings Cliffe became the centre of a royal park and many Tudor mansions were built in the village. Sadly little evidence of these remain.

KINGS SUTTON

This was Sudstone in 1086 – the south tun (farmstead) in relation to the village of Purston, which was far more important in Saxon times than was this village. The estate was taken over by William the Conqueror towards the end of the 11th century, thus causing the name to change to Sutton Regis. The present name did not appear until recent times.

Astrop, which is now adjoined to Kings Sutton, was the village of Estrop in 1200 and Astethorp in 1316. This derived from east thorp (village) and probably began life as a Scandinavian secondary settlement, an offshoot of Sutton. In the 18th century it became Astrop Wells, an important spa resort.

Purston, already mentioned, was Prestetone in the Domesday Book. This was originally a tun (farmstead) belonging to a preost (priest). The separate settlements of Great and Little Purston developed in the Middle Ages, the latter growing as the colonial or daughter village to the former.

Southwards from Kings Sutton is the hamlet of **Walton Grounds**. This was listed as Waleton in the Domesday Book, possibly being a corruption of weall-tun (wall farm). The settlement stands on the old **Port Way**, once a main road coming north from Aynho to Banbury. A 'portway' was a market road – a way that led to a market town.

In the 7th century, legend tells us, St Rumbald was born here at Walton Grounds. He was the son of Penda, the pagan King of Mercia. The baby declared his belief in the Trinity, gave long sermons on theological philosophy and asked to be baptised. He then died – at the age of just three days! **St Rumbalds Well** in King Sutton is, of course, linked also to this legend, being used for baptisms.

Close to Walton is **Twyford Farm**, a name derived from the Saxon twy meaning 'two'. Thus, there was a double ford here.

Kings Sutton is a large attractive village, set around a pretty green and towering church. **Lovells** in the Square is named after the lords of the manor in the 14th century, and the **Butchers Arms**, which dates back to the 17th century, was once a combined pub and butcher's shop. The latter subsequently moved next door. **Whittall Street** was once called High Street and **Red Lion Street** was named after a former inn, now a general shop.

KISLINGBURY

Through the Middle Ages the spelling of this name changed frequently, from Cifelingeberie (1086) to Kiselingeberia (1175), Chilesengebur (1247) to Keselingbury. The most likely derivation is from three separate Saxon words: ceosol (gravel), inga (people of) and burh (fortified place) – 'the fort of the gravel dwellers'. The settlement stands on the Nene meadows, just west of Northampton, where the soils are indeed sandy with alluvial deposits. There is an alternative theory that the prefix comes from a personal name, Cysel, but no firm evidence supports this. The change from the initial C to the present K probably arose out of Viking influence.

The **Cromwell Cottage**, a restaurant and pub, was originally three cottages. It is said Oliver Cromwell stabled his horses here in 1645 the night before the battle of Naseby. The stables used were close to the churchyard. **Bly Lane** could be so called from the old name for the stream here. One old medieval document mentions the Aquam de Blythe, that is, the Blyth Water.

South of Kislingbury is **Hill Farm**. This is not named from an upland site but from Dionis de Hulle, who held the manor in medieval times. **Hollowell Hill Farm** is derived from halig wielle (Saxon for 'holy well' or 'holy spring'), and **Stockall Farm** is from stocc wielle (Saxon for 'stump well', or 'spring by the tree trunk').

■ LAMPORT

This was once a lang (long) port (market town). It probably grew up along a Saxon trade route linking Rothwell and Northampton. The Saxons used the word port (from the Latin porta for 'gateway') to mean any settlement which provided an entry – into a gap in the hills, into a district or distinct farming region. Thus port invariably came to mean 'trade centre' or 'market town'. In the Domesday Book (1086) the village was called Langeport, in 1553 Lamperd.

The **Lamport Swan** inn is so called because swans figured in the coat of arms of the Isham family, which once owned Lamport Hall.

To the east is the vanished village of **Faxton**. This was Fextone in 1086 and Faxtona in 1166 – probably derived from Faecce's tun (farmstead). The Black Death reduced the village to a hamlet in the 14th century. Four hundred years later the Ishams, who owned the estate, removed the remaining houses to make way for sheep grazing. The church, however, did not disappear until 1958.

Hanging Houghton was Hohtone in 1086, clearly from hoh-tun, the Saxon for 'farm on a spur of land'. The adjective was added in the 13th century, as Hangende. The village is sited on the edge of a steep slope.

LAXTON

This might have come from the Saxon Leaxa-inga-tun 'the farmstead of Leaxa's people' or else more simply Lax's tun (farm). Etymologists believe the personal name Leaxa or Lax was Scandinavian and used as a nickname. Lax was also the Viking word for 'salmon'. The early spellings include Lastone (1086), Laxetona (1130) and Lextone (1226).

To the south-west is **Spanhoe Farm** and **Spanhoe Wood**. The origin here could be the Saxon spon (chip of wood or length of timber) and hoh (ridge or projection of land). Thus the name could have meant 'woodland spur'.

Laxton Hall, a fine classical building, is now a private school.

LILBOURNE

This little place is sadly wedged between the M1 motorway and the A5 road, standing in the shadow of the Rugby radio station masts. In Saxon times it was an isolated hamlet, with only the river Avon for company. In the 11th century it was Lineburne and Lilleburne, deriving from Lilla's burna (stream).

Dow Bridge was Douuebrigge in 1330, a corruption of the meaning 'Dove Bridge'. Either doves were common here or the bridge belonged to someone called Duua. Interestingly, the word 'dow' is an old dialect word for a 'dove'.

LILFORD

From Lilleford (1086), Lillingford (1205) and Lillesford (1284) etymologists have suggested an origin from Lilla's ford. If this is true the question arises as to whether this Lilla is the same person who gave his or her name to Lilbourne, or whether Lilla was merely a common Saxon name. Lilford and Lilbourne are a long way apart!

Lilford Hall, built in the early 17th century, has been owned by the Powys family since 1711. Thomas Littleton Powys (1833-96) was a leading ornithologist. The **Lilford Owl** was named after this estate.

LITCHBOROUGH

Sometimes called Lichborough, this is thought by many people to be the Celtic garrison town Lycanburgh captured by the Saxons in AD 571. It could well be, for the ancient fortifications of Castle Dykes and Stow Heath are not far away, and some evidence has been found of Celtic settlement.

The early spellings of Liceberge (1086), Lickesberga (1176) and Lichebarue (12th century) suggest a suffix from beorg (burial mound or hill) and a prefix either from licc (stream) or lica (body). So the place could have been 'stream by a hill' or, more interestingly, 'hill of the dead'.

Radmore Farm, north-eastwards towards Bugbrooke, was Redmor in the Middle Ages. This came from read (red) or hreod (reed) and mor (moorland or upland).

LODDINGTON

This was originally Lodda's ingtun (farmstead). In the Domesday Book of 1086 it was Lodintone, in 1299 Lodynton and in 1305 Ludington.

The school here was once the home of the Allicocke family.

The village of **Orton** was Overtone in 1086 and Oreton in 1283. This came from the Saxon words ofer (slope or bank) and tun (farmstead).

LONG BUCKBY

Buckby has two possible origins. Either it comes from the by (Viking for 'farmstead' or 'village') belonging to a tribal leader named Bukkr, or else it derives from the 'by where deer were found'. Bucc was Saxon for a 'buck' or 'male deer'. In the Domesday Book (1086) the name was Buchebi, this later changing to Bukebi (in 1175) and Bokeby (in 1264). It did not become Long Bugby until 1565, by which time the village had developed a linear shape.

Up to the 18th century the village had prospered with the weaving and spinning industry, a factor which led to the regular celebration of the feast of St Blaze (Blaise), the patron saint of woolcombers. The boot and shoe industry also developed here. Rail and canal links further boosted growth. The latter led to the development of wharf facilities down at the canal two miles away. Craftsmanship also created employment in narrow boat fitting and the gaily-painted utensils used on such vessels are still called 'Buckby cans'.

Many of the names in and around Long Buckby recall the village's past. The castle has gone but its site can still be seen. The estate was owned by the de Quincy family in the 12th and 13th centuries, thus linking the village with the Earls of Winchester.

Cotton End takes its name from the Saxon word cot for 'cottage'. To the south-west is **Holborough Hill**. This was Houberwe in the 13th century, a corruption of holh (hollow) and beorg (hill). The hill here is almost cut in half by two deep hollows.

Near Long Buckby Wharf is **Surney**, where there is a bridge and lodge. This was once Southeney, a name originating as south eg (southern island). The place is surrounded by rivers.

Greenhill Farm was the home of Simon de Grenehille during the Middle Ages; and **Ryehill Lodge** was Ryenhull in the 13th century. The sandy soils here were good for growing rye. Other local names include **Murcott**, which derives from mor-cot (the cottage in the wasteland); **Leighton Lodge**, a corruption of leactun (vegetable enclosure or garden), and **Rockhall Hill**, originally Rokwelhyl meaning 'rock-spring-hill'.

LOWICK

This was Ludewic in the Domesday Book, probably deriving from Luha's wic (farm). During the 12th century it was variously listed as Lufuuich, Hluwic and Luffewyk, and in 1262 it was Lowike.

The church of St Peter has a well-known lantern tower, visible for miles around. The nearby pub, the Snooty Fox, was formerly called the White Horse. The parish hall, once the village school, is known as the **Germain Rooms**, after Lady Betty Germain, of nearby Drayton House, who was a philanthropist during the 18th century.

Outside the village is the famous **Lowick Oak**, one of the largest trees in the country.

Drayton House to the south-west of Lowick, stands on the site of a medieval village called Draiton. This name derived from draeg (sloping land over which boats were dragged) and tun (farmstead). The estate has been owned by various families, including the Greenes, the Mordaunts and the Sackvilles.

Bullicks Wood was just called Bulex or Bolax in the 13th century. This is thought to have come from the Saxon words bula (bull) and exe (pasture). Interestingly, there is also, north of Lowick, **Oxen Wood**.

LUDDINGTON-IN-THE-BROOK

Much of this village was built in 1863 by the Duke of Buccleuch, who owned most of the land hereabouts. Indeed, the Buccleuch Estate still owns large parts of north-east Northamptonshire. Interestingly, it is thought this name derives from Lulla's (or Lilla's) ingtun (farmstead) – the same personal name that produced the place-names Lilbourne and Lilford. Historians still have not discovered the identity of Lulla. In the Domesday Book this village was simply called Lullintun. In the 13th century it was Lylington and Lollinton. The present elongated version appeared for the first time in the 15th century, as Lodyngton in the Brooke.

The river here is the Alconbury Brook.

LUTTON

This village is also known as Luddington-in-the-Wold but Lutton has become more common in recent years to distinguish it more clearly from Luddington-in-the-Brook, just a little way to the south. In the 10th century it was Lundingtun, and in the Domesday Book Luditone. In 1428 both names were recorded: Lutton and Ludington. The derivation is thought to be Luda's ingtun (farmstead).

The 17th century manor house was once the home of the Apreece family.

Papley was Pappele in the Middle Ages, from Pappa's leah (clearing).

■ MAIDFORD

Historians do not know why a village like this should be named after a maiden – in this case 'maiden's ford'. Perhaps it was the site of an ancient nunnery, or maybe it was associated with pagan fertility rites. Alternatively, an early church here was possibly dedicated to the Virgin Mary.

Some etymologists say that the prefix in this name does not come from maegden (Saxon for 'maiden') but from maegth (mayweed) or maere (boundary). It has even been suggested that it comes, instead, from mere, the Saxon for 'lake' or 'pond'. The early spellings vary from Merdeford (in 1086) and Maideneford (in 1166) to Maydenford (1285) and Madeford (1359).

Nearby **Burntfold Copse** could be so named because the area was originally cleared by burning.

MAIDWELL

As with Maidford this name probably derives from maegden, Saxon for 'maiden', but could, alternatively, come from other Saxon words, like those for 'mayweed' and 'boundary'. The suffix is from Saxon wielle for 'spring'.

In the Middle Ages this manor was divided into two, having two churches and two manor houses. One of the churches (St Peter's) was demolished in the 16th century, its site now being occupied by **St Peter's Close**. The demolished manor house stood near **Manor Farm**. The surviving manor house became Maidwell Hall, now a school.

The village hall is called **Loder Hall**, after R.B. Loder the last lord of the manor who died early in the 20th century. North of the village is **Scotland Wood**. The name probably derives from the old word scot meaning 'a payment' or 'tax'. In medieval times a rent was paid by anyone wishing to cut wood from a forest.

Berrydale Covert was Burghdale in the Middle Ages, from burh (fortified place) and dael (valley).

MARSTON ST LAWRENCE

Originally this was just Merestone (in 1086) or Merston (in 1181), a name derived from mersc-tun (marsh farm). Later the dedication of the parish church was added, giving us, in 1330, Mersshton sci Laurencii.

The Blencowe family owned the estate from the 15th century onwards. Close to the church is the **Marston Yew**, a tree thought to be 1,000 years old. **Costow House** is a name corrupted from the Saxon cot (cottage) and stow (place). **Dean Barn** stands in an area once owned by the Dean and Chapter of Lincoln Cathedral.

MARSTON TRUSSELL

The early spellings, Mersitone in 1086 and Merston in 1220, probably derived not from the Saxon mearc for 'march' or 'boundary' (despite the village being situated close to the Leicestershire border) but from mersc, the Saxon for 'marsh'. It was the marsh tun (farmstead). The Welland meadows are prone to flooding even today. The appendage appeared in medieval times; Osbert Trussell leased the estate from Henry II in the 12th century. His grandson Richard became lord of the manor in the following century.

The village used to be known as 'Pudding Poke Marston' as the road through it was a cul-de-sac ending at a place called Pudding Poke. Poke is an old word for 'bag'. One corner of the churchyard is called **Cavaliers Grave**. After the battle of Naseby a group of Cavaliers were cornered here, and subsequently slaughtered by the Roundheads.

MEARS ASHBY

Like other Ashby place-names this derives from aesc (Saxon for 'ash tree') and by (Scandinavian for 'village'). It was Asbi in 1086 and Essebi in 1166 but became Essebi Mares in the 13th century to distinguish it from all the other Ashby villages in Northamptonshire. Robert de Mares held the manor from 1242. By 1297 the name had become Mares Assheby.

The **Griffins Head**, formerly the Boot, shows the Stockdale family crest on its inn sign. The Stockdales have owned the hall since the late 18th century.

The village school was originally set up through the generosity of Sarah Kinlock, the sister-in-law to an 18th century vicar. She left money and land in her will to pay for the education of local schoolchildren.

Incidentally, it is said to be unlucky to count the number of lanes in the village – there are 13 of them.

MIDDLETON

This village is now joined to Cottingham, close to the Leicestershire border. It was called Middelton in 1197 and Middilton in 1285 – clearly from middel-tun, the Saxon for 'middle farm'. It was probably so called because it was between Cottingham and East Carlton.

Swinawe Wood was Swinehawe in 1203, derived from swin-haga meaning 'swine enclosure', that is, a pig pen. **Yokewood Lodge** was called Yoke Wode in 1535. This woodland was evidently used for making animal yokes.

MIDDLETON CHENEY

Mideltone (1086) and Midelinton (1215) were spellings obviously derived from middel-tun (middle farm). In order to distinguish this village from the Middleton in the north of the county, it became Middelton Curcy in 1224. At that time the estate was owned by John de Curci, but in the previous century it was held by Simon de Chendut.

The village was the 'middle farm' between Purston and Wardington in Warwickshire. The village of Lower Middleton Cheney appeared later in the Middle Ages, as the village grew.

Overthorpe was thorp (secondary settlement) standing on a hill above Banbury. The **Halt** comes from the Saxon word for 'wood'.

The **Moors Drive** housing estate was the site of one of the first battles fought in the English Civil War during the 17th century.

MILTON MALSOR

In this name Milton is a relatively modern corruption of Middleton and indeed until quite recently the place was also known as Middleton Malsor. The present name arose to avoid confusion with Middleton and Middleton Cheney. In the Domesday Book it was just called Mideltone – the middel-tun (middle farmstead). It stood between Rothersthorpe and Collingtree. In the early 13th century the estate was owned by Henricus Malaopera, whose surname was Latin for 'ill works' (mal opera). This later changed to Malesoures and the present addendum is a corruption of this.

The manor house was once the home of Sir Sapcotes Harrington, whose son James wrote *Oceana* in 1656.

Next to the Greyhound pub is the old Malt House belonging to the Hope Brewery, which stopped making beer in 1892.

MORETON PINKNEY

Originally this would have been the 'farm by the marshy place' – in Saxon, mor-tun. By the time of the Domesday Book, however, it had become Mortone. During the 13th century the two names Geldene-mortone and Gilden Moreton were recorded, possibly from the Saxon gylden meaning 'golden' or 'wealthy'. These later gave way to Moreton Pynckney in the 16th century. The Pinkeni or Pinchengi family was first mentioned in the 11th century. This name probably derived from Picquigny in Picardy. The family came over to England with the Norman invaders.

To the east is the farm called **Canada**, this either being an ironic name for a distant settlement or else commemorating Dr Oxendon, a local man, Metropolitan of Canada 1869-78.

Beyond here is **Plumpton**, once a plum farm.

MOULTON

This could derive from Mula's tun (farmstead) but is more likely to come from mul-tun (the 'farm where mules are kept'). There is no record of a tribal leader in this area called Mula, but mules were commonly used by the Saxons as beasts of burden. The early spellings of this place name include Multone (in 1076), Multon (in 1086) and Molentun (in 1205).

Now almost a northern suburb of Northampton, Moulton is well known for its links with William Carey, who was pastor here before founding the Baptist Missionary Society in 1792. The Jeyes family also lived in the village. The brothers Philadelphus and John set up a company making their invention, Jeyes fluid disinfectant.

Thorpelands was so called from the word throp, meaning 'outlying village' or 'dependent farmstead'.

The pub name **Artichoke** is shared by only two other pubs in England.

■ NASEBY

This is where, in 1645, the most decisive battle in the Civil War was fought. Cromwell's Roundheads defeated Charles I's Cavaliers in a conflict which claimed nearly 2,000 lives. The battlefield is just north of the village. **Prince Ruperts Farm** recalls the commander of the Royalist forces.

Naseby originated as a Saxon name but was later altered by the Vikings. In the 11th century it was recorded as Navesberie, probably taken from a Saxon personal name, Hnaefe, and the Saxon word burh for 'fortified place'. By the 12th century, however, it had become Nauesbi, the prefix having been changed to Nafni and the suffix to by (village) both being Scandinavian elements. In 1253 it was recorded as Naveneby.

Naseby is a quiet, unassuming village, with a museum, two pubs and a grid-pattern street plan. The lane called **Gynwell** is named after a cleric in the Middle Ages, and the **Fitzgerald Arms** remembers the Fitzgeralds, who owned much of the estate in the realy 19th century. Nearby **Avon Well** is the source of the river Avon, which later flows through Shakespeare's Stratford-upon-Avon.

Shuckburgh Farm, to the west, was Shukbourgh in 1540, named from the family of Thomas Shukburgh who owned the land.

NASSINGTON

This name comes from three Saxon words: naess (ness or headland), inga (people of) and tun (farmstead). So it would have been the 'farm of the headland dwellers'. The village stands on a small promontory above the river Nene. In the 9th century the name was Nassingtona and in the Domesday Book it was Nassintone.

The village has links with nearby Peterborough Cathedral, the ancient manor house once being a prebendary. It is thought King Canute held a manor here and a Saxon cemetery has been found. The Black Horse pub dates from the 17th century.

To the north-west is **Great Byards Sale**. This was Bayard Sale in 1726. In the Middle Ages it was owned by William Avenel de Biart. The word sale could come from the Saxon word sealh (willow tree) but is more likely to come from a local dialect word for a division of forest land.

To the south-east is **Lyveden Farm**. This was once owned by William de Lyveden from Lyveden near Brigstock.

NEWNHAM

This was simply the neowe ham (new homestead), and possibly dates from the late Saxon period, built after other settlements nearby had already been founded. In 1020 it was called Newaeham, in 1166 Neuenham and in 1255 Neweham.

The 17th century manor house was owned by the Thornton family, having previously been held by the Knightleys of Fawsley. The **Romer Arms** is named after Romer Williams, who settled at Newnham Hall in 1898. When a previous pub, the Bakers Arms, was destroyed by fire he kindly offered to finance the rebuilding programme. In consequence he became a much loved local.

There are numerous springs and wells in and around Newnham, many of whose names still survive. These include **Codwell Spring** in Tanners Field (on the Staverton road) which is a corruption of 'cold well'; **Narbrook Spring** on the Grange estate; **Coppid Moor Spring** near the Nene brook, and **Langhill Spring** on Newnham Grounds. Coppid Moor derives from the Saxon word cop meaning 'cap', indicating that the trees here had been capped (pollarded). The spring in Butts Ley was named after the Reverend Thomas Cotton, who paid for the repair of the watercourse. **Butts Ley** was the place where archery practice took place in medieval times.

Manor Lane was formerly called Dyers Lane and Low Street; **Mounts Lane** was once called Markers Lane after a 14th century inhabitant; and **School Hill** was Hill Street. The road from Upper Green to the Staverton road was named **Horns Lane**, after the family once living there, and **Perkins Way** (as well as **Perkins Farm**) recalls a common Newnham surname during medieval times.

NEWTON

This is also known as Newton-in-the-Willows. In the late Middle Ages there were no less than three villages here, called Great Newton, Little Newton and Barford. There was also a manor house, owned by the Tresham family. Today all that remains is a small hamlet, a redundant church and a dovecote.

The original settlement, Newetone in 1086 and Niwenton in 1162, was the neowa-tun (new farm). In due course it prospered and set up a daughter village, called Little Newton. The original became Great Newton. Then Barford appeared, the name coming from baerlic-ford (barley-ford – the ford over which barley was carried). All three settlements thrived. Then the landscape was enclosed and sheep were grazed over the entire estate. By 1700 only Little Newton survived. Later the 'Little' was dropped and 'in-the-Willows' was added. There is still a **Barford Lodge** towards Rushton.

NEWTON BROMSWOLD

This was just Niwetone in the Domesday Book, deriving from neowa-tun (new farm). The first mention of Bromswold appeared in 1605. The origin of this second element is interesting. Bromswold was the name of a stretch of woodland that covered the borderlands of Northamptonshire and the old county of Huntingdonshire. It derived from the Saxon brom (thorny bush) and weald (forest). At the other side of this woodland is Leighton Bromswold.

NORTHAMPTON

Hamtun, which was the spelling in AD 917, was the Saxon word for a 'main farm' or a 'chief manor' in a district. It was more than just a ham or a tun, both of which, on their own, meant 'farmstead' or 'homestead'. A hamtun was usually the biggest and most important settlement in an area. By the 11th century this place-name had become Northhamtun and Northantone, the prefix having been introduced to distinguish this town from Southampton, to which it was linked by an ancient routeway.

Many of the district names are in fact the names of old villages and hamlets that were separate farming communities throughout the

Middle Ages. Up to Tudor times Northampton stretched no further than the river Nene to the south and Upper Mounts to the north. In the west the Norman castle, at the top of what is now **Castle Lane**, formed the edge of the built-up area; to the east the town finished at Beckets Park (also known as Cow Meadow).

Kingsthorpe was the King's torp or throp (outlying farm). The king in question was a Saxon monarch. From just Torp in the Domesday Book it became Kingestorp by the 12th century. **Kingsley** was linked to Kingsthorpe, being the healh (plot of land), owned by the same Saxon monarch. It was called Kingeshala in the Middle Ages.

Abington is a corruption of the Saxon Abba's ingtun (village) and was called Abintone in the Domesday Book. Further out was a place called west tun (west farm) because it was west of Little Billing. This became Westone in 1086 (a district name still preserved) and Wesson Favell after the 13th century, when Hugo Fauvell owned the manor. It was not so long ago that the area around **Weston Favell** was covered in cherry orchards – a fact remembered by the **Cherry Orchard Estate**. Next to this is **Booth Lane** leading to **Boothville**. There was a Booth Farm hereabouts which was called Buttocks Booth before the Victorians cleaned the name up. The Scandinavian word, both, meant 'temporary shelter' and such a building, usually a wooden or stone hut, is still called a bothy in mountainous areas.

The Nene meadows south of Weston Favell were once covered in reeds and rushes (hence the name **Rushmere**). This area was not well inhabited, but cottages were dotted around, their medieval residents living off fish and dairying. **Cotton End** and **Far Cotton** are both place-names deriving from the Saxon word cot meaning 'cottage'. Coton is a corruption of coten, the Saxon plural form. In due course hamlets developed around these cottages. Far Cotton was once known as West Cotton.

Delapre was the site of an abbey first mentioned in 1217. It was then called Sancte Marie de Prato. Later on in the Middle Ages this changed to De La Preez, then to Dalapray and finally to De La Prey. Incidentally, the original name Prato was from the Latin pratum meaning 'meadow'. Preez was actually a corruption of the Norman French word for meadow, pred.

Delapre was not the only religious establishment in old Northampton. On a site now occupied by the Express Lift Tower stood St

James' Abbey. This was founded in the 12th century by William Peveril as a house for the Black Canons of Augustines. This became a very large and powerful monastery, until destroyed at the Dissolution. The **St James** district preserves many names recalling this past – **Peveril Way**, **Abbotts Way**, **Abbey Street** and so on. There were two other religious houses in those days – one friary for grey friars (on the site now occupied by **Grey Friars Bus Station**) and another for white friars.

Further out from central Northamptonshire are other place-names with an interesting history. **Hunsbury Hill** to the south-west, is an Iron Age camp. It was called Hunsbarow in 1712, a name deriving from a Saxon personal name, Hunna perhaps, and burh meaning 'fortified place'.

Semi-Long has had a convoluted development as a name. It was Southmyllywong in the 15th century, which was an evolution of suth-myln-vangr meaning 'south-mill-enclosure'. **Lumbertubs** has a prefix from the Saxon word lumm meaning 'land by a pool', and a suffix possibly linked with an old word for a wooden vessel. The district is drained by a tributary of the Nene.

Some place-names may not be found on any map but are none the less real and with interesting derivations. One example is the district known as The Boroughs, another is the area nicknamed Paddy's Meadow.

The Boroughs is that district between St Andrews Road and Horse Market and surrounding Mayorhold. Some say the name is corrupted from 'burrows' since the area was highly populated with jumbled houses built close together, like a rabbit warren. Others maintain that the name comes from the fact that the Borough Yard (council depot) was situated in the area (in Bath Road). Here town rubbish was collected and burned in large furnaces, making the houses blackened with smoke. A third possible origin of the name is that the district lies within the original 'Borough', that is, lies within the old town walls. The old castle formed the south-west corner.

Paddy's Meadow lies to the west of The Boroughs, and is bordered by Spencer Bridge Road, St Andrews Road and the river Nene. Years ago this area had lush water meadows leading down to a wide stretch of the river. This became a favourite haunt for swimmers. In due course crude facilities were provided, changing huts, drying areas and lifebelts. A keeper was appointed to act as an unofficial lifeguard, an Irishman called Patrick Moore, known to everyone as 'Paddy'. And popular he became. He organised swimming lessons for children, ran competitions and races, and awarded prizes out of his own pocket. Sadly, the 'baths' were closed during the Second World War and the river subsequently became clogged with weeds. But the name 'Paddy's Meadow' survived.

Pleasure gardens of an earlier period were sited west of Paddy's Meadow. These were called **Franklins Gardens**, a name that will be found on a map. Originally called Melbourne Gardens (after Lord Melbourne, who owned land here in the early 19th century) they were purchased in 1886 by John Campbell Franklin. There was a swimming pool, sports pitches and refreshment facilities. People used to travel out from Northampton at weekends and on bank holidays to enjoy the relaxed atmosphere and fun provided. In the early 20th century a public company purchased the gardens and extended them over Abbey Gardens.

Another open space long enjoyed by locals is **Beckets Park**, east of the old Cattle Market. This contains a children's playground and various sports facilities and is also known as Cow Meadow. Cattle used to graze here prior to auction at the market. The park is named after Thomas à Becket, Archbishop of Canterbury from 1162 to 1170. There is a story that, after his escape from Northampton Castle, after his trial, he stopped at a well to refresh himself. That well, now called **Beckets Well** stands on the other side of Bedford Road.

South of Beckets Park is **Nunn Mills**, a site now occupied by the Avon factory. The original mill was demolished in 1970. The spot is named from the convent at Delapre, the nuns coming down to the river here to wash and fish. Further upstream are the sites of many other mills. **Cotton End Mill** was once called Marvells Mill, a corruption of an early owner by the name of Mervin, **St James End Mill** was called Samwell Mill in the 16th century, since it was owned by the Samwell family.

Amongst the old street names in Northampton there are many which indicate the trades or craftsmen that once inhabited premises there. The **Drapery** was where cloth was made, this street being called Le Draperye in 1540. Before then only the west side was called the Drapery. The east side was called the Glovery. **Mercers Row** was the street where dealers in silks and velvets were located. **Gold**

Street, **Tanner Street** and **Woolmonger Street** have self-explanatory origins.

Medieval towns had numerous markets and fairs, and even with these, different trades used to segregate. **Mare Fair** and **Horse Market** both dealt in horse auctions; **Sheep Street** was the site of the sheep market and **Wood Hill** was where woodmen from the surrounding forests could set up their stalls and sell furniture, wooden tools and carved trinkets. **The Parade**, on the north side of Market Square, was once called Cornhill. Nearby was Osborne's Jetty, formerly Fishmongers Row.

Derngate was originally the name of one of the town gates. The prefix derives from the Saxon word dierne meaning 'secret' or 'hidden'. The gate was possibly located in a dip in the landscape.

College Street was named from a house belonging to the collegiate clergy of All Saints, founded in the 14th century. **Beakward Street** is a corruption of 'bear ward' – a keeper of performing bears. Bears were a common sight in the Middle Ages. This road was called Berwardstrete in 1324. **Newland** was Le Newland Strete in 1540. It was built after the Grey Friars priory was established in 1245 and so named because it covered land previously undeveloped – that is, farmland.

Many streets, like **Angel Lane**, are named after the pubs located along them. But many of Northampton's pubs have names that are interesting in their own right. Some pubs, like the **Clicker**, are named after the old trades of the town. In this case a 'clicker' was a man who cut leather for shoe uppers. Northampton, of course, grew rich on the boot and shoe industry. Other pubs have names of more curious derivations. The **Bull and Butcher** was once the Sun and Raven and the Kings Arms. The present name is taken from the butcher's shop that used to stand next door. The cattle market is not far away. The **Mailcoach** was formerly the Swan. It was renamed soon after the post office was built nearby. The **Red Rover** (once the Red House) is close to the old tram terminus.

The **Princess Alexandra** was named after the Prince of Wales' wife at the time it was built (1880), the **King Billy** was built during the reign of King William IV. The **Garibaldi** remembers the hero of Italian unification in 1861. The pub was probably named when he was in the news.

Finally a last word on Northampton's sports teams. The football team is nicknamed the 'Cobblers' for obvious reasons – because of the town's historic connection with boots and shoes. But the reason why the rugby team is nicknamed the 'Saints' is less well known. Originally the team was set up by the curate of St James' church who wanted to keep the local youth away from potential crime. At first the team was called the St James Football Club, and it was then that the nickname was coined.

NORTON

This was simply the north tun (farmhouse) associated with the village of Dodford. In the Domesday Book it was Nortone. This is a quiet stone built village just east of Daventry. The row of cottages known as **Tattle Bank Row** is said to have been named from the gossiping inhabitants. In the early 19th century the owner of Norton Hall, Beriah Botfield, had a mistress, who frequently called. Hence the gossip. Legend says that Botfield even had the old village demolished and rebuilt further from the hall, to give his mistress more secrecy. Most of the present village dates from Victorian times. The hall, however, was demolished in 1947.

To the north of Norton is **Thrupp Grounds**. This was originally thorp, an 'outlying hamlet'. To the south is **Noborough Farm**, once called Norburgh. This would have been either north burh (fortified place) or north beorg (hillock). **Mazedale Spinney** is a name derived from maere (boundary) and dael (valley).

On the far side of the Grand Union Canal is the hamlet of **Muscott**. This was Miscote in the Domesday Book, Musecot in 1202 and Mosecote in 1268. It is thought this name comes from the Saxon musa-cot (mouse cottage). Either this was a nickname for a small humble abode, or it meant the cottage was infested by mice.

There was a Roman town in this vicinity called Bannaventa. Legend tells us that it was here that St Patrick, patron saint of Ireland, spent his early life. Born in AD 389 in Wales he moved here when a baby.

■ OAKLEY, Great and Little

Now situated on the outskirts of Corby these two villages once stood in the heart of Rockingham Forest – a location that led to their name. Oakley, as might be guessed, derives from the Saxon ac-leah (oak clearing). In the Domesday Book it was Achelau and in 1166 Achele. By the 13th century, two separate villages had appeared, known as Ockele Magna and Ockele Parva (from Latin for 'great' and 'small').

Great Oakley Hall, home of the Capell Brooke family for over 500 years, stands a little distance from the village. In the 19th century Arthur de Capell Brooke helped to found both the Royal Geographical Society and the Travellers Club.

Monks Well, in the grounds of Bridge Farm in Brooke Road, was associated with nearby Pipewell monastery (now disappeared). **Oakley Purlieus**, and to the west, **Carlton Purlieus**, recall the Norman French word purlieu. This denoted a tract of land on the edge of a woodland.

OLD

The present spelling is quite recent, for old county books (and the oldest inhabitants) call it Wold. And this tells us its origin, for it comes from the Saxon word weald meaning 'woodland' or 'high heathland'. In the Domesday Book (1086) it was Walda, in 1316 Wolde.

The landscape here, south-west of Kettering, is undulating and once famous for sheep grazing. In appearance it is not dissimilar to the Cotswolds and Lincolnshire Wolds.

OLD STRATFORD

Historically this village is part of Stony Stratford, which stands across the Great Ouse in Buckinghamshire (now being engulfed by Milton Keynes). To distinguish this end from its neighbour it was called Westratford in 1278, Forstratford in 1330 and, finally, Oldstratford in 1498.

Stratford is a corruption of the Saxon stret-ford – the street crossing a ford. The Saxons often used the word stret to mean a Roman road. In this case we have Watling Street (now the A5) which ran from London to Wroxeter, thence to Chester.

At the end of the 19th century a light railway ran from Wolverton to Deanshanger via Old Stratford, and some evidence of this can still be found. There was also, once, a windmill towards Passenham, now recalled by the name **Windmill Field**. Another field is called **Chapel Close**. This was the site of an old chapel and hermitage, later used as a leper hospital.

Shrobb Lodge Farm takes its name from the Saxon word scrybb meaning 'scrub', 'brushwood' or 'shrub'.

ORLINGBURY

Here the bury suffix comes not from burh (Saxon for 'fortified place') – as might have been expected – but from berg or beorg (Saxon for 'hill' or 'mound'). The prefix is taken from a personal name, Ordla or Ordin perhaps. Hence we have Ordla's hill. In 1086, in the Domesday Book, it was Ordinbaro, in 1131 Orlinberga, in 1388 Orlibergh.

In the church is a 14th century effigy to Jock or Jack Badsaddle, reputedly the man who killed the last wild boar in England (in some accounts, the last wild wolf). He came from a village long gone but still remembered in the name **Badsaddle Wood**, west of Orlingbury. This village was Batisheshell in 1313 and Battsadle in 1556 – derived from Baetti (a personal name) and haesel (hazel or hazel clump). ·

OUNDLE

An interesting name this, for it comes from the name of a Saxon tribe that lived in north-east Northamptonshire soon after the Romans left England. It is thought the name of this tribe was the Undalas, coming from the Saxon word undal meaning 'undivided'. This could indicate that the tribe was given land that had been 'left over' from earlier divisions of land ownership – that they had settled on open land unallocated and unfenced. The earliest record of this place-name was in AD 725 when it was Undolum. This later changed to Undola and Undele in the 10th century and Oundel in 1301.

Oundle is famous for its public school, and boasts a fine collection of old stone buildings and historic connections. One of the oldest pubs is the **Talbot Hotel**. Most pubs of this name recall the talbot hunting dog, a breed now sadly extinct. But this establishment was once called The Tabrot, possibly a corruption of the word 'tabard' – the sleeveless tunic worn by heralds.

The town centres on the Market Place. **St Osyth's Lane** was once called Lark Lane and leads down to **Herne Road** (linked to Herne Lodge). This derives from the Saxon word hyrne meaning 'loop'. This part of town stands within a large meander of the river Nene.

New Street was formerly Berry Street, once leading to Berrystead. This was Buristeede in Tudor times, from burh (fortified place) and stede (site of a building). **West Street** and **North Street** were once known, together, as High Street. **Ship Lane** was called Parva Venella (Little Lane).

Sadly two old street names have disappeared, Chapel End and Duck Lane. The former was situated on the site of a medieval chapel, dedicated to St Thomas of Canterbury, and stood just north of Milton Road. The latter had been Ducke Lane, a corruption of Dikelane in the Middle Ages, from the Saxon word dic for 'ditch'.

Also gone is Crowthorpe, or Crowethorpe, which was a corruption of crow-thorp (an outlying village where crows were seen).

Amongst the new street names, which commemorate past inhabitants, are **Latham Road** and **Wyatt Way**. Parson Latham founded the almshouses in North Street. Robert and Joan Wyatt founded a guild at the end of the 15th century, financed the building of the south porch in the church, and helped to establish a town school.

OVERSTONE

This comes either from Ofe's tun or from ofer-tun. Ofe might have been a Saxon tribal leader, ofer was Saxon for 'river bank', 'steep ridge' or 'embankment'. Tun meant 'homestead'. There are numerous streams in this part of the county, just west of

Wellingborough, so the meaning 'farm on a river bank' seems the more likely derivation. Early spellings include Oveston (11th century), Ouston (1275) and Overston (1284).

The present village was laid out in the 18th century outside the landscaped parkland of Overstone House. The original settlement stood near the manor house.

■ PASSENHAM

If it were not for the Great Ouse this village could well be a suburb of Milton Keynes. As it is, Passenham has retained something of its old charm. It was Passanhamme in the 10th century, a spelling that suggests an origin from Passa's hamm (meadow). The meadows here, in fact, were called Le Hamme for most of the Middle Ages, and since by many old inhabitants. In the Domesday Book the village was called Passonham, in 1277 Pasenham.

The church of **St Guthlac** dates from pre-Norman times. Guthlac was born in about AD 673 into the Mercian Royal Family. After an early career leading his Saxon army he entered a monastery at the age of 24, becoming a hermit two years later. He lived the rest of his life in the Fens, tending to the birds and beasts of the marshes. He died in AD 715.

There are many old roads in the village, **Boswell Lane** is named from the Buswell Brook, now flowing underground. This would originally have been Bosa's wielle (spring). **Church Lane** was once called Hospital Lane, since it led to an old leper hospital, and **Folly Lane** is a corruption of Foley Lane, where once stood a woodland shelter or cabin made out of foliage. **Patrick's Lane** is named after Richard Patrick, a local baker who built the cottages at the bottom end. **Shrob Walk** and **Lane** is a corruption of the Saxon word scrybb meaning 'scrub' or 'brushwood'.

PATTISHALL

Pascelle in the Domesday Book (1086), Patesshille in the 12th century and Patteshull in the 13th century, all suggest that the origin of this name is 'the hyll (hill) belonging to a person called Paetti or Pasca'.

This is a large village that grew substantially during the 19th century with the boot and shoe trade. That part of Pattishall adjacent to the A5 is called **Fosters Booth**. This could be a corruption of 'Forsters' Booth' but is more likely to be a corruption of 'foresters booth'. Whittlewood Forest, now lying some distance to the south, once stretched this far. It is thought there was a shelter here then, used by foresters and huntsmen, on a site later occupied by an inn called 'Foresters Booth' (now Peggotty's Restaurant). Nearby **Debdale Flats** comes from the Saxon deep dael – deep valley.

PAULERSPURY

The name used in the Domesday Book was Pirie, which was a corruption of the Saxon word pyrige meaning 'pear tree'. In those days this area was famous for its orchards. Later on, in the 13th century, the estate passed into the ownership of Robert de Pavelli (or Parueli). Subsequently the village became known as Paueleyespirye (in 1319).

During Tudor times the Throckmorton family owned the estate, and in 1761 William Carey the missionary was born here. During the 19th century the village became famous for its lace, which was much appreciated by Queen Victoria.

Plumpton End is named from plum tun (farm), just as **Pury End** might have been 'pear farm' (although the latter actually stands for 'Paulerspury end'). **Tews End** has a name taken from the family of Hugh de Tywe who once owned the estate. To the north is **Heathencote**, which is just south of Towcester. This was Heymundecot in the Middle Ages, from Heahmund's cot (cottage).

Cuttle Mill was once Cuttlebrok, suggesting Cuttel was the name of the brook. **Stockings Field** is from the Saxon stoccen, plural of stocc (stump). The field was evidently cleared by felling.

PIDDINGTON

Situated beyond the northern edge of Salcey Forest, this village grew substantially after the coming of the railway line. The station was at the southern end. Today any signs of the line have gone, but its course can still be followed.

Pidentone in the Domesday Book and Pedinton in 1166 suggest an origin from Pyda's ingtun (homestead).

In 1781 the missionary William Carey married a local girl Dorothy Plackett. The wedding took place in Piddington church.

PILTON

The present spelling first appeared in 1313. Before that it was Pilchetone (1086) and Pilkenton (1189). The origin is probably Pileca's tun (farmstead).

This is a small quiet place situated above the Nene meadows, and south of Oundle. In 1630 Erasmus Dryden married Mary Pickering here. They were to become the parents of John Dryden the poet. The manor house was owned by the Tresham family. North-westwards is **Bearshank Wood**. Robert Bareschanke rented this land during the 13th century.

Winning Foot Hill was called just Wininge in 1255. The Saxon word win meant 'got' or 'obtained' (hence our modern word 'win') and, in this case, probably indicated land claimed from the woodland. It was land newly 'won' for farming.

PIPEWELL

The pronunciation of this name – 'Pipwell' – closely resembles its derivation – from Pippa's wielle (spring). Pippa was probably a local Saxon leader. In the Domesday Book the spelling was Pipewelle, in 1177 Pippewell and in 1231 Peppewella.

There was once a rich and powerful monastery here, belonging to the Cistercian order. It was founded in 1143 and demolished after Henry VIII's Dissolution. Richard the Lionheart used to come to this abbey when planning his crusades. Today only humps in the fields around the village – and the local name **Monks Arbour Wood** – recall its existence.

Rawhaw Wood is a corruption of the Saxon words ra (roe deer) and haga (enclosure).

PITSFORD

The present village dates largely from the 17th century. The original settlement, located north of the church, was destroyed by fire in 1619. The early spellings included Pidesford (1086), Pittesford (1203) and Pictesford (1235) – these deriving from the Saxon Peoht's ford.

For a village once famous for its numerous springs – estimated at nearly 300 in the vicinity – it is perhaps fitting that the place should now be famous for its reservoir. This supplies much of the water for nearby Northampton.

The manor house was once owned by the banker Samuel Jones Loyd. The **Griffin** pub, in earlier times, was used by Welsh cattle drovers, on their way to the Northampton market.

Incidentally the present name Pitsford dates only from the 19th century. From the 14th century until then the name was Pisford. No doubt the Victorians changed it out of modesty!

POLEBROOK

Interestingly, this name comes from puca-broc, Saxon for 'goblin brook'. Either the stream here was mischievous, being prone to flooding, intermittent flow or course alterations, or else it possessed some mystical, pagan or sinister quality. In the Domesday Book the name was Pochebroc, in 1203 Pockebroc, in 1254 Polebroc.

To the south-west towards Barnwell is **Armston**. This was Armestun in 1140, deriving from Eorm's tun (farmstead). **Kingsthorpe Lodge**, eastwards of there, was so called because the estate was owned by Saxon royalty – the thorp (outlying village) of the king.

Burray Spinney was Burweye in medieval times, deriving from burh (fortified place) and weg (way). It is thought this place was on an old trackway that led to a fort or moated settlement (perhaps Barnwell).

Coney Geer Coppice is a corruption of conyger meaning 'rabbit warren'. Rabbits were introduced into England by the Normans.

POTTERSPURY

This was called Perie, Pirie and Pery in the 11th and 12th centuries and, like Paulerspury a little to the north, derives from the Saxon word pyrige. This whole district was once famous for its pear trees. By the 13th century – to distinguish it from its neighbour – this village became known as Potterispirye, this soon evolving into Pottere Pyrye. At that time the place was growing as a centre for pottery making.

Potterspury is an interesting village with many old cottages and historic associations. **Blackwell End** was named from a blaec wielle (dark spring) and **Brownswood Cottage** is a corruption of Branteswyrth – Brants' worth or the worth (clearing) created by brand ('burning').

The **Old Talbot** pub is named after an old breed of hunting dog (now extinct), and the **Cock** is thought to be so named because part of the building was once used as a butcher's shop.

The area to the west was once covered by the dense woodland of Whittlewood Forest. This became a royal hunting estate in the Middle Ages, many trees being felled to create animal runs. Within this forest stood Wacafeld, a settlement name corrupted from Waca's feld (open land or enclosure) and now known as **Wakefield**. During the 18th century the Dukes of Grafton lived at Wakefield Lodge. The manor house was redesigned by William Kent and the parkland was re-landscaped by 'Capability' Brown. Sadly the estate was later broken up, and sold in 1918.

To the east of Potterspury is **Furtho**. This village largely disappeared in the 17th century as a result of enclosures and sheep grazing. Only the church, a dovecote and a farm mark the site. It was called Forho in the Domesday Book, and Fortho later in the Middle Ages. The name comes from ford-hoh – the 'ford near a projecting ridge or spur'.

PRESTON CAPES

This was simply called Prestetone in the Domesday Book and Prestona in 1174 – from preost tun (priest farm). In the 13th century, however, two settlements were beginning to grow up, the colonial or daughter village appearing a little to the south-east. To distinguish the two, the names Magna Preston and Parva Preston were used. These were later changed to Preston Capes and Little Preston respectively. Hugo de Capes, from a Norman family, held the estate in the 13th century and his name was subsequently added to that of his village.

An ancient trackway – some say a Roman road – runs through Preston Capes. This is the **Portway**, a name meaning 'market road' or 'trade route'. It linked Daventry with Brackley.

To the west is **Cleaver's Clump**. This is named after the family of Richard Cleaver, who owned the land in the 17th century.

PYTCHLEY

This comes from the same personal name that gave us Pitsford – Peoht. Either this Saxon owned land at both villages, or he was a tribal leader that controlled much of the region between Northampton and Kettering. Here we have Peoht's leah (clearing) which became Pihteslea in AD 956, Picteslei in 1086 (in the Domesday Book), and Pyghtesle in 1316.

Pytchley Hall was built originally by the Isham family in 1580. During the 18th century it became the home of the Pytchley Hunt, the hounds being kept in the outbuildings. When the hall was demolished in the 19th century, however, the Hunt headquarters and kennels moved to Brixworth. But **Isham Road** still survives to recall the old hall and its first owner.

The **Overstone Arms** is named after the Lord and Lady Overstone who once lived at nearby Overstone House. They were great philanthropists during the 19th century.

Cox's Lodge is probably so named because Thomas Cox of Kettering owned land here in the 17th century.

■ QUINTON

The early spellings, Quintone (1086), Quenton (12th century) and Quynton (13th century), suggest that this name comes from Cwena's tun or Cwenena tun. Cwena was a common Saxon female name and cwenena was a word used for woman. So this settlement began as a farmstead owned by a particular woman, or by a group of women. In Saxon times women had a much higher status in society than they did in the Middle Ages, and, indeed, could run farms and make land-ownership contracts. Incidentally, it is from the Saxon root that we get our modern word 'queen'.

■ RADSTONE

Etymologists have not yet decided about the exact derivation of this name. The prefix could come either from rodu (clearing) or from rod (cross); the suffix could be either from stan (stone) or from tun (farmstead). Thus, we might have the various meanings 'stone in a clearing', 'farm in a clearing', 'cross farm' and 'stone cross'. The early spellings do not actually help in deciding the most likely. In 1086 it was Rodeston, in 1200 Roddestone, in 1225 Rudeston.

Coldharbour Farm is a common place-name. It derives from the Saxon hereberwe which was used to mean a 'place of shelter for wayfarers', a 'roadside refuge'.

RAUNDS

This town is largely a product of the 19th century and Victorian industrialisation. It grew with the boot and shoe trade and with brick making. In the Middle Ages there was just a small settlement here – called variously Randa, Randes and Rawns. The earliest known spelling is Randan in AD 980. It was Rande in the Domesday Book (1086).

The Saxon word rand meant 'edge' or 'boundary', and so this place-name evolved probably because of the location of the village near the Bedfordshire border. Years ago a local form of marble was quarried here, called Rance Rag. This name preserves the old pronunciation of Raunds.

The pub name **Worlde Upside Down** originated with an 18th century landlord called Silas Coggin. He was so disorganised that customers never knew where anything was kept, including the beer.

Just to the south of the town is **Darsdale**. In the Middle Ages this was the home of Gilbert de Deresdale. **Knighton's Row** was named after the family of Thomas and George Knighton, who lived here in the 17th century. **Midland Road** and **Station Road**, of course, recall the time when a railway line ran from here to Bedford and Peterborough; nearby **Butts Road** is named from an earlier period when 'butts' were archery ranges.

To the east is the ancient site of **Mullows Cotton**. This is an old encampment or village. Cotton is a corruption of 'cot' or 'coten' (cottage, cottages). There were many cot place-names in this area during the Middle Ages: Parva Cotes, Media Cotes, Wylinecotys and, in this case, Mullecotes. The last named was probably Mulla's cot originally.

RAVENSTHORPE

This does not come, as some people have thought, from raven's thorp – the thorp (village) where ravens are seen. Instead it comes from Hrafn's thorp. Hrafn was a personal name. Thorp, or throp, not only meant 'village' but also 'dependent farmstead' – that is, a settlement which grew as an off-shoot of a larger and more important neighbour.

Curiously the spelling of this name in the Domesday Book was closer to the present version than subsequent spellings. In 1086 it was Ravenestorp but this later changed to Raunestorp (1247), Rounsthorp (1486) and Ransthorpe (1539).

RINGSTEAD

This would have been hring-stede originally, Saxon for 'circular place' or 'ring site'. It was so called either because it was built in a hollow (a natural depression), or else because the settlement itself was round in shape. The name has not changed much over the years. In the 12th century it was Ringstede, in the 13th century it was Ringsted and Ringestede.

In the middle of the 19th century the village hit the national headlines with the murder here of Lydia Atley. The local butcher, William Weekley Ball, was suspected of the crime but was never convicted.

ROADE

The pronunciation of this name has probably never changed, although the spellings have. In the Domesday Book it was Rode, in 1402 it was Roode and in 1629 Rhode. It has been suggested that the name derives from rad – Saxon for 'road' – since the village stood on an ancient trackway. This is not likely to be true, however. Instead it comes from rod, Saxon for 'cleared land' or 'open woodland'.

In the 16th century the estate was held by the Mauntell family.

Early in the 20th century the village greatly benefited from the presence of Sir Cyril Cripps. He owned the local Pianoforte Supplies. With his wealth he financed the football team, built two pavilions, one for the cricket team and another for the bowls team, and donated two new bells to the church.

Thorpewood Farm was Thrupp Wood Farm in 1662. This was a corruption of thorp or throp meaning 'dependent farmstead'.

ROCKINGHAM

The village nestles below the hill upon which stands Rockingham Castle, the medieval fortress which has been inhabited almost continuously since Norman times. But the name of this village has nothing to do with the rocky outcrop that forms the castle's foundations. Instead it comes from Hroca-inga-ham: the homestead of the people of Hroca. The Domesday Book records the name as Rochingeham, this later changing to Rogingham (12th century) and Rokingham (13th century).

The 17th century pub, the **Sondes Arms** is named after the family which owned the estate in the Middle Ages. Since Tudor times the castle has been home to the Watsons, who have done much to

preserve the character of the village. Richard Watson, in the 19th century, modernised the cottages, financed the village school (now the village hall) and helped restore the church.

ROTHERSTHORPE

The prefix here could originate from the Saxon word hryoer meaning 'cattle' but is more likely to come from the Scandinavian personal name Rethaer. The suffix derives from thorp or throp meaning 'village' or 'secondary settlement'. From just Torp in 1086 and Throp in 1226 the name became Ritheresthorp in 1242 and Rothers Thrupp in 1675.

In the centre of the village is the **Berry** or **Bury**. This is the site of an Iron Age camp. The name is from the Saxon word burh meaning 'fortified place'.

The pub called the **Chequers** recalls the time when the monks from St James Abbey, Northampton came to the village to collect rents from their farm tenants. They would do their sums with the aid of a chequered counting board. Such a system was common in the Middle Ages. Because of this, any treasury would be called an 'exchequer' and the person in charge of the government's finances became known as the Chancellor of the Exchequer.

North-east of the village, close to the M1 motorway, is **Brook Farm**. This was the home of Richard Attebrok in medieval times.

ROTHWELL

It was once thought the prefix here derived from the Saxon word read, or Scandinavian word rauthr, both meaning 'red'. But it is now thought to come from the Saxon rothu (or rod) for 'clearing'. Thus we have a name meaning 'spring in a clearing' and not 'red spring'. The suffix is from the Saxon word wielle, for 'spring' or 'well'. In the Domesday Book (1086) the place was Rodewelle, in the 12th century Roewella, in the 13th century Rothewell. The 16th century spelling was Rowell – still the local name for the town.

The annual Charter Fair, held since 1204, takes place during the week following Trinity Sunday, the parish church being Holy Trinity.

The manor was held by a succession of noble families after the Norman Conquest: The Clares in the 12th and 13th centuries, the Earls of Stafford in the 15th century, the Treshams in the 16th century. The last named is commemorated in **Tresham Street**. Sir Thomas Tresham (1545-1605) built the Market House and the nearby Triangular Lodge. His son, Francis, was involved in the Gunpowder Plot.

In the early Middle Ages Rothwell was surrounded by a town wall, through which were several gates including East-bar and West-bar. **Castle Hill**, it is thought, derives either from the site of a fortified manor house built by one of the early manorial owners, or else from the site of a gatehouse in the town wall. Other street names reflect Rothwell's later history. **Crispin Street** is named from the old Crispin Works, Rothwell's main shoe factory – St Crispin being the patron saint of footwear.

Ragsdale Street commemorates Owen Ragsdale, the Rothwell schoolmaster who endowed the grammar school and founded the Jesus Hospital almshouses towards the end of the 16th century. **Shotwell Mill Lane** led to Schotewelle in the 13th century, derived from sceota (Saxon for 'trout') and wielle (Saxon for 'spring', 'well' or – as in this case – 'stream'). The site of the old mill can still be seen.

Sun Hill was named after the Sun Inn, now called the Rowell Charter Inn. **Well Lane** once led to the Lady Well, a spring of pure water famous in medieval times for its healing powers. St Mary's

Chapel, a shrine built there, was demolished at the Dissolution in the 16th century.

John Smith Avenue was named after a missionary sent to British Guiana by the London Missionary Society and **Ponder Street** was named after Nathaniel Ponder. He was born in Rothwell (1642) but moved to London where he set up a printing press. He printed the first edition of John Bunyan's *Pilgrim's Progress*.

RUSHDEN

Risdene in 1086 and Rissenden in 1109 suggest to etymologists that this name comes from the Saxon words ryscen or rysc (rushy or rush) and denu (valley). By the 13th century the name had become Russenden, by the 14th century Russedene.

The Normans built a hunting lodge here, on a site later developed into Rushden Hall by John of Gaunt. He was the Lord of Higham Ferrers Castle and the hall was intended to house the royal hunting keeper. And it was around this site that the settlement of Rushden grew.

By the 15th century it had grown into a small town. Robert Pemberton, who served Queen Elizabeth I, settled here and rebuilt the hall. During the next three centuries the estate passed through other hands, notably the Ekins, the Fletchers, the Williams family and the Sartoris family. Many of these names live on in the modern streets: **Pemberton Street**, and **Sartoris Road** for example.

Lace making flourished here during the Middle Ages but it was not until the 19th century, with the coming of the boot and shoe industry, that industrialisation really took place. Expansion was rapid and by 1900 Rushden 'New Town' had been finished. To a large extent it had become a factory town.

The street names reflect this history of growth. **Duck Street** (possibly a corruption of 'ditch' street) was once Pungs Lane and **College Street** Higgins Lane after an early inhabitant. **Crabb Street** was named after a crab apple orchard that stood hereabouts, and **Newton Road** was once Church Lane. **Rectory Road** was a lane named Back Way, running behind the cottages in the High Street.

George Street was formerly Chapel Lane and Dentons Lane. Dentons was a shoe factory early in the 20th century and there is now a **Denton Close** on the eastern side of town. **Spencer Road** is part of the Spencer Park Estate. The Spencers of Althorp own land all over Northamptonshire. **Fitzwilliam Street** is named after G.C.W. Fitzwilliam who built Station Road and Wentworth Road.

An older name is **Tollbar**, at the junction of the A6 and A45 roads. There was a toll-gate here, erected in 1780 to stop people avoiding toll payments when travelling between Bedford and Barton Seagrave.

RUSHTON

As with the name Rushden, the prefix here derives from rysc meaning 'rush'. It was the rush tun (farmstead). Either it was a dwelling built in a rushy area or else it was a farm growing rushes, perhaps for

thatching. In the Domesday Book the name was Risetone, in 1293 it was Ryshton and in 1343 Russhton.

The **Thornhill Arms** is a pub named after an early lord of the manor. Not far away is the **Triangular Lodge**, the famous folly built by Sir Thomas Tresham in the 16th century. This building has three sides, three floors and three of all other architectural features (or multiples of three) – all in recognition of the truth of the Trinity. Sir Thomas was an ardent Catholic.

West of Rushton, near Desborough is **Gaultney Wood**. This was Galklynt in the Middle Ages. It is thought this was derived from two separate Scandinavian words galti (boar) and klint (steep slope or bank). To this, the Saxons added the suffix haeg meaning 'enclosure'. Thus, Gaultney comes from a name that meant 'sloping enclosure where boars are found'.

Storefield is from the Saxon storth (brushwood or young plantation) and feld (open space or enclosure). In the 13th century it was called Le Stordh.

■ SCALDWELL

This name is from the Saxon words sceald (shallow) and wielle (spring). There are numerous rivers around here, many now flowing into Pitsford Reservoir, and springs are abundant, rising up from the underlying limestone. In the Domesday Book the spelling was Scaldeswelle and in 1241 Schaldewell.

This is a pretty village with honey-coloured stone cottages. George Clarke, the 19th century antiquary, is buried here.

Roseholm was Rosholmbroke in 1345, being a compound word from the Viking hross (horse) and holmr (island) and the Saxon word broke (brook). Horses were once grazed here.

SIBBERTOFT

Here a prefix of Saxon origin (the personal name Sigebeorht) is followed by a suffix of Viking origin (toft or topt meaning homestead or smallholding). By the time of the Domesday Book Sigebeorht's toft had been shortened to Sibertod. In the 13th century it was Sibetoft.

In the late 19th century much of the land here belonged to the Villiers family, which lived at Sulby Hall (demolished in the 1950s). Elizabeth Mansell, Lady Villiers' niece, financed the building of the reading room in 1911, in memory of her two brothers who were killed in the army.

In Victorian times the vicar of Sibbertoft was Miles Joseph Berkeley, botanist and fungi expert who had a genus of algae named after him.

Castle Yard still shows signs of the motte and bailey that once formed the foundation of a Norman castle. **Moot Hill** was the site of an old meeting place, the name coming from the Saxon mot for 'meeting' or 'assembly'. **Dust Hill** was Dusthil in 1291, so named either because of the dusty soil here or from the Saxon word dus meaning 'heap'. This could have referred to a burial mound. **Westhorpe Lane** was once called Cattle End. At the bottom stood a mansion that was demolished in the 19th century.

West of Sibbertoft is the deserted village of **Sulby**. This was Solebi in 1086 and Sulleby in 1347, probably derived from sulh-by (furrow-farm), although some people think it might have been Sula's by. An old abbey stood by the river. The village disappeared as a result of the Black Death, enclosures and sheep grazing.

SILVERSTONE

The early spellings, Silvestone (1086) and Sulvestun, could indicate a derivation from the Saxon silvre-tun (sunny farm or silvery farm) but etymologists think this is incorrect. They say the name is a corruption of Siulf's tun, Siulf being a shortened form of the personal name Sigewulfe. The 1484 version Sylson is similar to the traditional pronunciation of this name.

Challock Farm marks the site of Charlock, a village that disappeared after the Black Death in the 14th century.

The famous motor racing circuit has many names that recall the past landscape. **Abbey Curve** is close to the site of Luffield Abbey, a medieval monastery. **Maggotts Drive** commemorates Maggotts Moor Lodge, a gamekeeper's cottage situated near one of the entrances to Whittlebury Forest, then a hunting park. **Chapel Curve** is named after an old Methodist chapel. This stood in a hamlet called Chapel Green, where there was once a medieval chapel said to have been visited by Thomas à Becket – hence the modern name **Becket's Corner**. A small woodland, Chapel Copse, is now remembered by **Copse Corner**. All these old sites were covered by a war-time airfield in 1939.

SLAPTON

Recorded as Slaptone in the Domesday Book and Slepton in the 13th century, this comes from the Saxon words slaep (slippery slope) and tun (farmstead). The settlement was built on a steep or damp river bank.

Francis Gostrell was born here in 1662. He became Bishop of Chester.

SLIPTON

The name was Sliptone in the Domesday Book of 1086 and Sliptun in the 12th century. Some people think this is from the same root as Slapton – slaep-tun (farm on a slippery slope). However, it is more likely to come the Saxon slip-tun (farm on a muddy surface or slimy farm). A few etymologists even think the prefix could derive alternatively from slipe, Saxon for a 'strip of land'.

SOUTHWICK

This was the suth wic (south farm) in relation to Apethorpe. It was probably a dairy farm since wic was used by the Saxons to mean a specialist farm and this area was once famous for its dairy herds. In

AD 980 the village was Suthwycan, in 1131 it was Sudwic and in 1275 Sothewyk.

The **Shuckburgh Arms**, a 16th century pub, was purchased from the Southwick estate by George Capron in about 1840. It was named after Capron's cousin, the Reverend J. Shuckburgh. The Caprons were the third family to own the beautiful 14th century Southwick Hall. Before them were the Lynnes and, previous to them, the Knyvetts (in the 13th century).

North-west of the village is **Morehay Lawn**. This was Morhey in 1249, a corruption of mor (marsh) and haeg (enclosure). Nearby is **Blackmore Thick Farm**, which was Blakemerethycke in the Middle Ages – the black-mere-thicket.

East of Southwick is **Perio Mill**, on the river Nene. This was Piriho in the 13th century, deriving from pyrige (pear tree) and hoh (spur of land).

Other local names of interest include **Crayley Wood** which is a corruption of grey leah (clearing); **Tottenhoe Lodge** which was Totta's hoh (spur of land), and **Old Sale**, a name taken from the old dialect word meaning a division of land. Southwick once belonged to the priory of St Mary of Huntingdon, and Old Sale was an area subdivided by the monks.

Park Colsters was Colestertis in 1286, a name derived from col (charcoal) and steort (piece of land). Charcoal was once burned here for fuel.

SPRATTON

There are two spellings for this name in the Domesday Book: Spretone and Sprotone. By the 13th century it had become Sportton and the present spelling first appeared in 1613. The name derives from the Saxon spreot (pole) and tun (farm). It was, possibly, a settlement where poles were cut and made – for use in building, as oars for punting, or in fencing.

Nearby **Broomhill** is a corruption of brom-hyll – a hill where broom grew. On the road to Northampton is an eminence locally known as 'Hungry Hill'. This name comes from the days of horse-drawn carriage transport. It was here that the carrier, his wife and passengers used to stop for lunch.

Westwards is **Teeton**. This was Teche in 1086 and Tetene in 1316 – from the Saxon tacn meaning 'signal' or taecne meaning 'beacon'. The high ground here was once used as a look-out point.

STANFORD-ON-AVON

Close to the county border – Stanford Hall is in Leicestershire – this lovely little village stands on the same river Avon that flows through Shakespeare's birthplace. The spelling has changed little over the years – Stanford in 1086, Stanfort in the 12th century – but the river name was not added until the 16th century. The origin is stanford, Saxon for 'stony ford'. The first village here was slightly north of the present village, moved in response to the demands of land ownership and changing farm practices.

To the north-east is the deserted village of **Downtown,** called Dura in Saxon times (from dun for 'hill'). This also suffered from the extension of sheep grazing.

Stanford Hall was built in the 17th century by the Cave family. In the grounds is a monument to Percy Pilcher, the pioneer aviator who crash-landed here in 1899.

Incidentally the name of the river is of ancient origin indeed – it comes from the Celtic word abona (similar to the Welsh afon) meaning 'water' or 'river'.

STANION

From stan (stone) and aern (building) this name suggests that the settlement began as a cluster of cottages around a stone storehouse – perhaps a place where grain was kept. The Domesday Book spelling was Stanere, this becoming Stanhern (1203) and Stanyerne (1481).

The pub, **Cardigan Arms**, is named after the Lords Cardigan of nearby Deene Park. The Brudenells – for such was their family name – owned much land in this part of the county.

A field near the church is called **Cowthick**, named from the legend of the Stanion Cow. This giant cow provided milk for the entire village, until killed by a local witch.

Corby Haw was Corby Hall Leys in 1560. Haw could be a corruption either of 'hall' or of haga (enclosure).

STANWICK

Stan Wigga (10th century), Stanwige (Domesday Book) and Stanewica (1209) all clearly suggest an origin from the Saxon words stan (stone) and wic (specialised farm). Either the farmstead was built of stone (unusual in Saxon times when most buildings were wooden) or it was located in a stony area.

Stanwick is an old village that grew in the 18th century with the leather and boot industries. The **Duke of Wellington** pub is so named because the Iron Duke's famous boots were made in a Stanwick workshop.

Dolben Avenue is named after John Dolben who was the son of the rector here. He became a writer, theologian and was appointed Archbishop of York after the end of the Civil War in the 17th century.

The village was also the birthplace of Richard Cumberland (in 1731). He was a poet and playwright. After his death in 1811 he was buried in Westminster Abbey.

STAVERTON

The prefix here comes from the Saxon staefer meaning 'staff' or 'pole' and from which we get our modern word 'stave.' The suffix is from tun (farmstead). Thus, the settlement was probably marked by poles originally, or surrounded by staves for defence. Early spellings include Staefertun (AD 944), Stavertone (1086) and Staveton (1460).

To the south, near Arbury Hill, is **Studborough Hill**. This derives from the Saxon strut-beorg (strife hill). The hill lies on the boundary of Staverton and Catesby parishes and its ownership might have been a bone of contention.

Elderstubbs Farm was obviously a place where elder trees grew. Stubbs were 'tree trunks' or 'stumps'. So the elders were evidently cut down.

STOKE ALBANY

William de Albini, who held this manor in the 12th century, had the village totally rebuilt on a grid pattern – producing the present network of Green, Middle, Chapel and Bottom Lanes. Henceforward the village name included his name. So from Stoche (1086) it became Stok Daubeny (1274) and Stoake Albane (14th century). Stoke is a corruption of either stoc (monastery, religious place) or stocc (trunk, stump). Since this village is close to Pipewell where a great monastery once stood, the former origin could be the more likely.

The village was the home of Lord Chief Justice Thomas Denman in the first half of the 19th century. He defended the Prince Regent's wife, Queen Caroline, against charges of immoral conduct in 1820.

STOKE BRUERNE

Stoche (1086) and Stokes (1220) became Stokebruere in the 13th century in order to distinguish this village from other Stoke villages in the county. William Briwerre held the manor in the reign of King John. Stoke is a corruption of stoc (religious place) or stocc (trunk).

Since the village was located on the northern edge of Whittlewood Forest the latter is more likely.

West of Stoke Bruerne is **Shutlanger**. This was Shitlanger before the Victorians changed it out of modesty. In the 12th century it was Shitelhanger – derived from the Saxon words scytel (shuttle or bolt) and hangra (hanging wood or wood on a steep slope). It was possibly a wood where shuttles were cut to be used as gate bars.

STOKE DOYLE

In this case the Stoche of the Domesday Book and the Stokes of the 12th century became Stoke Doyly in the 14th century, so that this village could be distinguished from Stoke Albany and Stoke Bruerne. John de Oyly held the manor in the late 13th century.

This part of Northamptonshire was once densely wooded, and nearby Oundle was the centre of various religious communities. Therefore the Stoke in this name could equally derive from stocc (tree trunk) or stoc (monastic site).

The church is dedicated to St Rumbold, who was born near King's Sutton, at the far end of the county, and the pub is called the **Shuckburgh Arms** after the family that once lived at Southwick Hall not far to the north.

Hatchdoyle is a modern corruption of Hatchdole. This derived from the Saxon haecc (hatch or gate) and dal (portion, usually of a common field). It is the latter Saxon word, incidentally, that gave us the word 'dole' meaning 'portion' or 'amount'.

STOWE IX CHURCHES

There is a Church Stowe and an Upper Stowe, and the latter was once called Butter Stowe, as a London carrier collected butter here. But in early medieval times there was just Stowe. The Saxon word stow had various meanings: 'place', 'holy place', 'hermitage', even 'church'. In 1418 we first come across the name Stow-with-the-Nyne Churche, which has given us the present name for the parish.

One story is that this name arose because nine churches could be seen from the hilltop. Another story tells how the Saxon builders tried eight times to build the church at the bottom of the hill, only to find a mysterious force moving the stones to the top of the hill. On the ninth occasion the builders erected the church on the hilltop, as demanded by the spirit. Neither story, sadly, is true. The name actually comes from the fact that the lord of the manor had right of presentation to nine local churches.

A castle once stood on the hill near St Michael's church. The estate was owned by the Danvers family in late medieval times and later by the Turner family.

Ramsden Corner Plantation has nothing to do with ramson (wild garlic). It was Ramboldesdene in the 10th century, a corruption of Raegenbeald's denu (valley).

SUDBOROUGH

This was the suth burh (south fort) in relation to Brigstock. In the 11th century it was Suthburhc and Sutburg, in 1249 it was Subburg. The burh need not have been a fort in the conventional sense. It could have been any site fortified – a hilltop camp or earthwork, a moated farmhouse or a castle. There is in fact an earthwork nearby, called **Money Holes**. This was not a 'fort' but a medieval monastery. Legend says that treasure is buried here.

Round Lown Wood was Round Lounds, from the old Norse word lundr meaning 'grove'.

The village pub, the **Vane Arms**, is named after a local landowning family.

SULGRAVE

This same spelling was used in the Domesday Book, although other spellings later appeared: Solegrave in 1294, Sulegrave in 1150 and Solgrave in 1300. The derivation is from the Saxon words sulh (channel or passage) and graef (pit or trench). The village was sited on a low spur in a broad deep-cut valley.

Barrow Hill probably comes from burh (fortified place) since it is

the site of an ancient earthwork. **Park Lane** was originally Dark Lane, and **Stockwell Lane**, which leads to an old pond and water mill, probably comes from a spring or well used for watering cattle.

At the northern end of the village is Sulgrave Manor, for which this place is famous. This was the home of the ancestors of George Washington, first president of the United States.

SUTTON BASSETT

In the Domesday Book, 1086, this was just Sutone – from suth-tun (south farm). It was so called probably because of its position in relation to Weston-by-Welland. In the 12th century Richard Basset, Chief Justice of England, owned the manor. Henceforward the village was known by the present name.

The Methodist chapel was built in the late 19th century as a memorial to the Sedgeley family.

SYRESHAM

Etymologists think that the 1086 spelling, Sigresham, was a corruption of Sigehere's ham (homestead). In the 15th century the village was called Siresham.

Abbey Way leads across the county border to Buckinghamshire and Biddlesden Park, where there was a medieval abbey. **Monks Wood** is named from the same connection.

To the east is **Earl's Wood**. The Earl of Leicester held this land in the time of Henry II (the 12th century). Beyond is **Wetley's Wood**. This was Weteley in 1287, being a corruption of wheat leah (clearing). **Hoppersford Farm** once belonged to the family of Thomas le Hoppere of Steane, and **Shiplands Copse** is a corruption of 'sheep's lands copse'.

SYWELL

This model village was built by Lady Overstone (of the Loyd family) in the 19th century. Today it is more famous as the site of Northampton's local airport, a descendant of a wartime airfield where pilots were trained.

The original village was called Snewelle and Siwella in the 11th century, and Seywell in 1287. It is thought the origin was seofon wiellen meaning 'seven springs'. This part of the county has numerous springs and streams, a fact that has led to the building during the 20th century of many reservoirs.

Hayes Lodge, to the south, was Hayes in 1598, this being derived from haeg (meadow or enclosure).

■ TANSOR

The prefix in this name could come from a personal name, Tane, but is more likely to come from tan, the Saxon word for 'branch' or 'fork'. With a suffix from ofer meaning 'shore' or 'bank' we have a place-name meaning 'branching riverbank'. Tansor stands on the Nene, as it meanders towards Fotheringhay. It was Tanesovre in 1086 and Tanshore in 1320.

In 1819 local farmer John Cave gave a portion of his land to set up a charitable trust.

THENFORD

This would originally have been thegn's ford (thane's ford). A thane in medieval times was a lesser nobleman, a landowner ranking below hereditary peers. The early spellings include Teworde (1086), Tanford (12th century) and Tinford (13th century). The ford was over a tributary of the river Cherwell.

The 18th century manor house was once the home of Michael Woodhull, the translator of Euripedes.

THORPE MALSOR

The Domesday Book spelling of this name was Alidetorp – the ald-thorp (old secondary settlement). But this had changed to Thorpe Malesoures by the 13th century, named after the family which held the manor. By the 14th century this had been shortened to Thorp Malsore.

The Jacobean manor house here has been the long time home of the Maunsell family, a great naval family in Stuart times.

THORPE MANDEVILLE

From just Torp in 1086 this became Throp Mondeville by 1300. Thorp or throp was an 'outlying farmstead' or 'secondary settlement', in this case possibly once linked to Sulgrave. Documents dated 1252 give the name of the family that owned the estate as Amundevill.

The estate has been owned by the Humphrey family since the 17th century. Behind the Three Conies pub is **Dove Close**, along which are the Dove cottages. These recall an old dovecote that was once sited here, in gardens called the saw-yard.

Ox-yard, near the church, was named from the ox pond. In this area the Thorpe Feast was held every July.

The **Doctors Close** was once called Calves Close. It was named after Dr Deacle, who farmed the plot here. He kept calves in a field nearby, close to **Bull's Lane**.

135

THORPE WATERVILLE

This was just Torpe in 1199, derived from thorp or throp (secondary or outlying village). The present name comes from the medieval owner of the estate Ascelin de Waterville.

To the north, and across the Nene from Wadenhoe, is **Achurch**, sometimes called **Thorpe Achurch**. This was Asencircan in AD 980 and Asechirce in the Domesday Book; probably from Asi's church. In 1316 Thorp Hacchurch was recorded, perhaps after Achurch and its thorp had merged.

The Linches is corrupted from hlinc, Saxon for 'bank' or 'ridge'. There is a steep wooded slope here.

THRAPSTON

There are various spellings listed in old documents, including Trapestone (1086), Traspton (1202), Thrapeston (1225) and Tharpston (1533). The suffix clearly comes from tun, Saxon for 'farmstead', but the derivation of the prefix is more complicated.

Most etymologists believe that a change of initial letters has taken place. An early personal name, Draefst or Draepst, became Trapsta in late Saxon times, perhaps with Viking influence. Such an alteration was common. The Germanic 'drei', for example, became the English 'three'; the Germanic 'dreschen' became 'thresh'. So we have a place name that was Draepst's tun.

Thrapston grew rapidly in the 19th century with the growth of the leather and shoe industries and the coming of the railways. Bridge Street station opened in 1845 serving the London and North Western line; Midland Road station opened in 1865 serving the Midland line. The former took trains to Peterborough and Northampton, the latter connected Kettering with Cambridge.

Before the railway era **Midland Road** was called Denford Road. **Oundle Road** was once Titchmarsh Lane and **Chancery Lane**, Fair Lane. Along this latter thoroughfare stood the old manor house, demolished in 1967.

De Vere Road was named after one of the medieval lords of the manor and **Gales Lodge** remembers John Gale who held the manor in the 16th century. Mill Road was renamed **Oakleas Drive** by the Loakes and Pettit company which built houses here in the 1930s. 'Oakleas' is almost an anagram of 'Loakes'. **Cedar Drive** was so called because it led to Cedar House. This is now municipal premises but was formerly the Union workhouse and, at a later date, an infirmary. The building was erected in 1836.

TITCHMARSH

Originally this was Ticcea's mersc (marsh or swamp). Ticcea was probably a Saxon landowner or tribal leader and the 'marsh' probably referred to the Nene meadows which were (and still are) prone to flooding. Before the Normans came the village was called Tuteanmersc and Ticanmersc. The Domesday Book records it as Tircemerse and by the 13th century it had become Tichesmerse.

In Tudor and Stuart times the lords of the manor here were the Pickerings. Later the estate passed to the Powys family of Lilford Hall. Titchmarsh Hall has since been demolished.

Polopit, at the southern end of the village is a corruption of Puddle Pit. Further away, **Coales Lodge** takes its name from William Coles, who owned the land in the early 18th century. **Chequer Hill Coppice** was Cheker Garden in 1523, possibly so called because of its varied crops and plants. **Bidwell Farm** was Bidewell in the 13th century. This was probably a corruption of the Saxon byde (hollow) and wielle (spring) – a spring in a depression.

TOWCESTER

All places whose names end with cester, chester, caster or xeter go back to Roman times, since these endings derive from the Saxon word ceaster (from the Latin castra) meaning 'Roman camp'. Towcester is no exception. It stands on Watling Street, the old Roman road from London to Wroxeter, thence to Chester (a route now largely used by the A5). Under the Romans the town was called Lactodorum – thought to be a Latin version of an older Celtic name deriving from llaith (damp) and duro (fortress).

The Saxons called the place Tofeceaster, the prefix coming from the river Tove. In the Domesday Book it was Tovecestre and in 1294 Touchestre. By the 16th century it had become Tocester.

The old town centre is still dominated by the straight alignment of Watling Street, but leading off this are some interesting lanes and corners. **Malt House Court** stands on the site of an old brewery yard, where the old fire station used to be. **Gilbert Scott Court** (named after the famous Victorian architect) was the old council depot, and before that the old workhouse.

Of the pubs, the **Brave Old Oak** is one of the oldest, being 16th century. The **Folly**, which is 18th century, is possibly named after a foly or folie – a woodland hut or wayside shelter that stood here-abouts in medieval times. The **Pomfret Arms**, although modern, takes its name from a local family that owned land here. There is also a **Pomfret Road**.

To the north of Towcester is **Bury Mount**. There is a hill with the remains of a moat. The name comes from the Saxon burh meaning 'fortified place'.

Further north is **Caldecote**. This was Caldecota in the 13th century, derived from ceald (cold) and cot (cottage). **Easton Neston House** takes its name from the hamlet called Estanestone in the Domesday Book. This would originally have been Eadstan's tun (farmstead). The present name grew out of the medieval version, Estnestone, and confusion with the Saxon root est-tun (east farm).

North of here is **Hulcote**. This would have been hula-cot (hovel cottage) before becoming Halecote in the Domesday Book. On the far side are **Showsley Grounds** and **Nun Wood**. The former was Sewardeslega in the 12th century, being a corruption of Sigeweard's leah (clearing). The latter was Nonewode in 1287, a wood owned by the nuns of Sewardsley Priory.

West of Towcester is **Costwell Farm** which is a corruption of 'cress well' or 'cress spring' – watercress growing near the river Tove. It was Kerswell in 1247. South of here is the deserted village of **Handley**, called Hanlegh in the Middle Ages. This derived from the Saxon heah (high) and leah (clearing). It disappeared as a result of the Black Death and the extension of sheep grazing.

138

TWYWELL

This was originally twi (two) wielle (spring). In other words, the settlement grew up on a double spring. In 1013 it was Twiwel, in 1086 Tevwelle and in 1438 Tweywell.

The area known as **Blackwells Close** is named after an 18th century engineering firm called Blackwells, run by two brothers. They made clocks and winnowing machines.

In the 19th century the rector here, Horace Waller, was a friend of Dr Livingstone and the church still contains mementos of the great explorer and missionary.

■ WADENHOE

From Wadenho in 1086 and Wadeho in 1236 we can deduce a derivation from Wada's hoh. Wada would have been a Saxon tribal leader or landowner, hoh meant 'spur of land' or 'headland' – in this case a projection into the river Nene. This location probably gave protection in time of tribal conflicts.

Wadenhoe House was the home of George Ward-Hunt in the 19th century. He was Chancellor of the Exchequer and a local benefactor, who financed both street lighting and a local gasworks.

WAKERLEY

The prefix here probably comes from the Saxon word wacor meaning 'watchful' or wacra, 'the watchful ones'. The village overlooks the Welland valley and would have provided a good look-out position. The suffix comes from leah (clearing). In the Domesday Book it was Wacherlei, in 1282 Waukerle.

The **Exeter Arms** is named from the Marquess of Exeter. The Cecils have lived at Burghley House, near Stamford, since Tudor times but formerly lived at a manor house here. It stood in the field opposite where this pub now stands.

WALGRAVE

Waldgrove (1086) and Walgrava (1195) suggest an origin from weald-grafa, meaning 'woodland grove'. However, some people think the prefix instead comes from the name of the local village of Old (formerly Wold). But since Old itself derives from weald the difference between these derivations is technical.

This is a quiet village now but it once hummed with the noise of boot and shoe workshops, producing footwear for the British army. At **Hall Farm** are the remains of an Elizabethan manor house.

WANSFORD

Historically within Northamptonshire, this village now shares its allegiance with Cambridgeshire. It would have been wielm-ford originally: the ford by the whirlpool. The Nene has local eddy currents here. From Wylmesforda in AD 972 it became Welmeford and Wamesford in medieval times.

The **Haycock Hotel** is named after the legend of Barnaby, who fell asleep on a haycock and got carried away on the floodwaters.

WAPPENHAM

From Wapeham in 1086 it became Wapenham in 1203. The prefix is from a personal name, Waeppa, and the suffix comes either from ham (homestead) or hamm (meadow).

Westwards towards Helmdon is **Radmore Farm**. This was Redmore in 1247, deriving from read (red) or hreod (reed) and mor (moor or wasteland).

Towards Silverstone is **Blackmires Farm**. This was a 'black mere' or 'dark pool'. In the 12th century it was called Blakemerewode. The area is still well wooded. **Cockerell's Copse** was named after the family of Elizabeth Cockrill, who lived nearby in the 18th century. **Potash Farm** was where potash was once made into fertilizer.

WARKTON

The personal name that produced this prefix could have been Weorc, Weorce or Weorca, all of which are known to have been Saxon names. With a suffix from tun (farmstead) we find Werchintone in the Domesday Book and Wercheton in 1166.

The village was much loved by the artist Sir Alfred East of nearby Kettering. Much of it is owned by the Buccleuch estate, the Montagus living at Boughton House.

WARKWORTH

In the 12th century this was Wauercuurt, in the 13th century it was Warcworth, in the 14th century Warcourth. The suffix clearly comes from worth (enclosure or village) but the prefix could derive from three different Saxon words: Wauferce (a personal name), waeferce (spider) or waefre (wavering or unsteady).

There was once a castle here with towers and a tall gatehouse. In the 17th century it was converted to a manor house; in 1805 it was demolished. But some remains survive as a farm. **Huscote** is derived from Husa's cot and **Nethercote** from nether cot. These were 'cottages', the latter was so called because it was below Overthorpe, close to the Oxfordshire border.

Grimsbury was Grimberie in 1086, being derived from Grim's burh (fortified place); and **Franklow Knob Farm** was Frankelowe in 1543, from Franca's hlaew (mound or tumulus). **Spital Farm** is a corruption of Hospital Farm. There was once a leper isolation hospital here, the Hospital of St Leonard.

WARMINGTON

Originally this was either Wyrma's ingtun (village), or else Wyrma-inga-tun (Wyrma's peoples' farm). Wyrma would have been a local leader or landowner. Before it was Warmintone in the Domesday Book it was Wyrmingtun.

Eaglethorpe, down by the Nene, was Ekelthorpgrewe in 1297. This was the thorp (outlying farmstead) belonging to a person called

Ecgwulf. The manor house here is 17th century and contains some external woodwork from Fotheringhay Castle.

Eastwards is **Stock Hill**, corrupted from stocc (stump) and **Davey's Farm**, owned by Richard Davie in the 16th century.

WATFORD

This village gives its name to the Watford Gap service station on the M1 motorway. The Gap is a gap in the limestone hills. The present spelling was actually used in the Domesday Book, but Wadford and Wateford were used in medieval times. The prefix comes either from waed (wade) giving us 'wading ford', or else from wao (hunting) giving us 'hunters' ford'.

To the north is **Silsworth Lodge**, derived from Sifel's worth (enclosure or village). It was Silvesworth in 1213.

Burnums Farm, near the motorway, is named after Ralfe Burnham of Buckby, a landowner in the 16th century. **Langborough** is from long beorg (hillock) and **Rodmore Lodge** from hreod-mor (reed marsh).

WEEDON BEC

Different parts of this village are called Upper Weedon, Lower Weedon and Road Weedon; it has also been called Church Weedon, Weedon Royal and Weedon-on-the-Street. But in medieval times it was just called Wedon (1086), Weddona (1166) or Whedon (1252). These came from the Saxon weoh (shrine or holy place) and dun (hill). The present appendage came later, after the manor passed into the ownership of the monks of Bec Hellouin Abbey in Normandy.

The name Church Weedon arose from the fact that Weedon was once a great religious centre. A chapel and priory to St Werburgh stood on a site in an area called Ashyards. This was where the miracle of the geese occurred. St Werburgh stopped the birds eating the crops simply by preaching to them. She also brought one goose back to life after it had been eaten by a servant, the carcase becoming fleshed again.

The name Royal Weedon came about after a royal pavilion was built here, and a royal military depot. These were built to house and defend George III in the event of a Napoleonic invasion. Weedon-on-the-Street arose as a name because the village stands on Watling Street, a Roman road.

WEEDON LOIS

This was the weoh-dun (shrine hill) originally called Wedone (1086), Suthwedon (1261) and Wedune Pynkeny (1282) – south because it was south of Weedon Bec, and Pynkeny, because the manor was held by that family. A priory was founded here in the 12th century, first belonging to the Benedictine order then later to the Cistercian Abbey of Biddlesham in Buckinghamshire. During the 15th century a group of French monks brought to this priory the bones of their patron saint, St Lucien. Henceforward the village was called after that saint, the name being corrupted into Leyes, Loys and finally Lois. There is also a St Loys Holy Well nearby, its health-giving waters being used by pilgrims up to the 18th century.

Milthorpe, to the south, was Middiltrop in the 12th century – the middle throp (village) lying between Weedon and Weston.

WEEKLEY

Wiclea in AD 956 and Wicklea in 1194 obviously derived from the Saxon wic leah (specialised farm by the clearing).

Weekley Hall Wood was not named after a manor house but after a haga (fenced enclosure), a word which often became haw and, sometimes, hall.

Boughton House, home of the Dukes of Buccleuch, is located on the site of a hamlet called Boctone in the Domesday Book. This was from boc-tun (beech tree farm).

WELDON, Great and Little

Now a suburb of Corby, this was Walesdone in 1086, Welledon in 1166 and Waledon in 1234. The first mention of two separate villages came in the 16th century – Myche Weldon and Parva Weldon. The derivation is from wielle-dun (spring by the hill). At one time the village was called Weldon-in-the-Woods because it stood in the middle of Rockingham Forest.

The manor house at Great Weldon was owned by the Basset family in the Middle Ages and the Colet family in the 15th century.

Bangrave Wood was Barnegrave in the 13th century, coming from bern (barn) and grafa (grove).

Priors Hall was not a house or hall owned by the monks at Fineshade Priory, but a haga (fenced enclosure).

WELFORD

Once an important stagecoach centre, Welford became a busy canal village after being linked up to the Grand Union Canal. The **Wharf House** pub is a reminder of the canal trade that made the village wealthy in the early 19th century. The name was Wellesford in 1086 and Wileford in 1200, derived from wielle (spring) – the 'ford by the spring'.

To the south-west are the **Hemplow Hills** and **Hemploe Lodge**. Etymologists think the medieval form, Hindeplewe, was a corruption of hind-plaga: the 'hinds' play-place', or the place where deer played.

WELLINGBOROUGH

From the Domesday Book version, Wedlingeberie, we can deduce a derivation from Waendel (a personal name), inga (the people of) and burh (fortified place) – 'the fort of Waendel's tribe'. It was Wendlingburch in 1178 and Wellyngburgh in 1316.

It used to be thought that Wellingborough derived its name from the numerous wells which existed in and around town. It did not, but there are indeed many wells here, several of whose names still survive.

Red Well had health giving qualities and was once visited by Charles I and his wife, Queen Henrietta. There was also **Lady Well** (off Finedon Road), **Whyte Well**, Stan Well (otherwise known as **Stone Well**), Rising Sun Well and Bury Moor Well. Most of these now have roads named after them. There was also a Holy Well (or **Holly Well**) and a **Buckwell**. Many other wells were named in old documents but these have been lost – Hemming Well, Wheywell, Wichus Well. In 1830 no less than 30 wells were recorded just in the Cannon Street district.

It was not just wells that were common but also springs, pools and lakes, for Wellingborough has a very watery location. It stands close to where the river Ise meets the Nene, and many other streams flow down at this point. A scatter of street names indicate this: **Swanspool**, **Spring Hill**, **Brookfield**, **Well Street**, **Spring Gardens** and **Rock Street**, the last named after Rock's Pond.

Around **Croyland Park** are many names connected with the abbey thought to have stood hereabouts in the Middle Ages: **Abbots Way**, **Monks Way**, **Friars Close**, **Abbey Road** and **Priory Road**. The name Croyland comes from the Benedictine Croyland Abbey in Lincolnshire. The building here in Wellingborough was not a monastery as such but a hall or grange owned by Croyland Abbey. There was probably a chapel, a dormitory, a farm with outbuildings and a house used for study. The tithe barn off Sheep Street belonged to the hall, and it was here that crops were stored. Tenants paid a tenth of their output in rent to Croyland – tithe being from an old word for 'tenth'.

There was another ecclesiastical building in Wellingborough during the Middle Ages, the Hospice of St John, which stood in what is now **St John Street** (one of the town's oldest streets incidentally). This was an annexe to the St John Hospital in Northampton, founded in the 12th century. It had two wells of its own and possessed lands as far away as Rushden, Whiston and Walgrave.

Herriots Lane was once called Little Silver Street but before that was known as Apostles Pond Land, from its connection with the St John Hospice. **Hill Street**, near Croyland Road, was named after Shrine Hill, the site of a medieval cemetery. It is thought this too was connected with the hospice.

The hospice survived until the 19th century, but Wellingborough

Castle disappeared much earlier. With names like **Castle Lane**, **Castle Road**, **Castle Mews** and **Castle Fields**, there seems little doubt that a castle once stood on a site to the east of the town centre. Yet, strangely, no evidence survives of its foundations nor is there any documentary evidence telling us when it might have been built. Probably it was no more than a fort, put up to provide defence just for the immediate area. If it had been made of wood it might not have lasted long and would not have left much in the way of remains. As a temporary structure it may well have lasted no more than a century during Norman times.

In the **Hatton Park** district are various streets named after Sir Christopher Hatton, who held manorial lands here in the 16th century. He was Lord Chancellor under Elizabeth I and sponsored such explorers as Francis Drake and Martin Frobisher. There is still a **Hatton House** on Broad Green, and many Hatton street names behind, on land once part of the manor house gardens. The **Hind Hotel** was named from the hind passant d'or – the golden deer which formed part of the Hatton coat of arms.

Sir Christopher acquired the manor in 1576 but did not live here, preferring his estate at Holdenby House. But other people who have areas or streets named after them really did live at Wellingborough.

Appleby Gate was named after Galfridus de Apelby who lived here in the 13th century; **Brook Farm** was the home of Philip Attebrok at about the same time; **Pinder Road** remembers Paul Pinder, who was born in Wellingborough in 1565 and became Ambassador to Turkey under James I. **Vivian Road** commemorates the Reverend C.P. Vivian, who was vicar of the parish church 1815-41 and lived at Hatton Hall, his monogram being over the front entrance.

More recent inhabitants are remembered in the names **Askham Avenue** and **Mannock Road**. John Askham was born in 1825, the son of a cobbler. He taught himself to read and write and became a well-known local poet. He died in 1894. Edward 'Mick' Mannock was an airman in the First World War. Attached to the Royal Flying Corps he was reputed to have shot down the highest number of planes of any pilot. He was awarded the VC, DSO and MC but sadly was shot down and killed in 1918.

With the Industrial Revolution and the coming of the railways Wellingborough grew rapidly, as factories were built and rows of

Victorian terraces were laid out. **Brickhill Road** occupies the site of the old brickfields and brick-making works; the **Butlins Sidings**, off the Irthlingborough Road, was the site of the Butlins Blast Furnaces, which moved in 1861 from their original site in Cannon Street. British Leyland later took over the premises.

Midland Road was built in 1860 after the station was built serving the London-Midland Railway. Nearby a small estate was built by Adam Corrie, a Scottish lace dealer who owned land here. **Chester Road** was named from his wife's maiden name; **Chace Road** from his son-in-law's surname; **Colwell Road** named after the place where his daughter was buried and **Senwick Road** from the place in Scotland where his son was buried.

Many Victorian streets were named after great personalities of the day: **Victoria**, **Albert** and **Alexandra Roads**, of course, from royalty; **Stanley Road** remembers the explorer; **Newcomen Road** from the inventor; **Havelock Street** after the General and hero of the Indian Mutiny in 1857.

East of London Road there once stood Dulley's Baths, the Dulleys being the Wellingborough family which owned the brewery at the bottom of Sheep Street. The baths closed in 1918 but **Dulley Avenue** survives.

Sadly many old street names have gone. Market Street was called 'Le Chepyngstede' in the 14th century (from chipping meaning 'market'); Gold Street was Common Town Street and Townsend; High Street was Broad Street. Perhaps oddly the old name **Pyghtle** has survived. This derives from the Saxon word pightel meaning 'small enclosure' or 'croft'. There were orchards here once – remembered by the new estate names like **Plumtree Avenue** and **Cherry Avenue**.

WELTON

Waletone in the Domesday Book and Welleton (1174) suggest a clear derivation from wielle-tun (spring farmstead). The village stands on the limestone hills of western Northamptonshire, where there are numerous springs.

To the west is **Hobberill Farm**, which was Hoberhul in the Middle

Ages, a corruption of holh-beorg-hyll (hollow-mound-hill). **Cockle Farm** was Cockes Mede in 1312, probably derived from a personal name, and **Mickle Way** was Michelewellehul in medieval times, coming from micel-wielle meaning 'large spring'.

WESTON

This is also known as Weston-by-Weedon. It was the west tun (farmstead) connected to Weedon Lois. The present spelling was first used in 1162.

Armada House was built in 1588, the year the Spanish Armada was defeated. The Baptist chapel, built in 1791, is the oldest in the county. Before that date Baptists used Cathanger Farm for services and baptisms.

West Hall was inherited by the Sitwell family in the early 20th century.

WESTON-BY-WELLAND

This was the west tun (farmstead) connected to Ashley, near the Leicestershire border. After being called simply Westone in the Domesday Book, it became Weston Bassett (after the Basset family that held the manor in the 13th century) and then Weston by Welland.

The Wheel and Compass pub was once called the Carpenters Arms.

WHILTON

This name probably derives from the Saxon words hweogol (wheel) and tun (farmstead). The village stands on a circular shaped hill. It was called Woltone in the Domesday Book and Whywelton in 1282.

Whilton Locks developed as a canal-side settlement but is now dominated by the M1 motorway. Nearby Whilton Lodge is on the site of the Roman settlement of Bannaventa, youthful home of St Patrick of Ireland.

WHISTON

This was the tun (farmstead) of the Hwicce tribe. In Saxon times it was Hwiccintunae and Wichentonam but had become Wicetone by the time of the Domesday Book.

The church was built in 1534 by Anthony Catesby and is known as the 'jewel on a hilltop' such is its attractive tower.

The Moat House, in the village, once accommodated King John on one of his visits to Northamptonshire.

WHITFIELD

This stands near a bend in the Great Ouse river but its name does not derive from wiht, Saxon for 'bend' or 'curve'. Instead it comes from hwit meaning 'white'. Feld, of course, was an 'open space' or 'enclosed land' – hence our modern word 'field'.

The name was Witefelle in 1086 and Wittefeld in the 13th century. It was a white field possibly because the soils were light in colour.

WHITTLEBURY

This name, and Whittlewood Forest, come from the same root, the personal name Witel or Witela. This was probably a Saxon tribal leader and this village his burh or 'fortified place' – perhaps being the centre of his area of influence. In AD 930 it was Witlanbyrig, in 1086 Witleberia. The present spelling first appeared in 1316.

The site of Whittlebury Lodge and its garden is now covered by a housing estate. It was once owned by the Dukes of Grafton, and later by the Lords Southampton and the Lees family, one of whom, Geoffrey, was a great philanthropist. The Lodge itself was rebuilt in 1865 but later was destroyed by fire.

Cattlehill Wood was Cattwell Hill in 1672, derived from 'cat wielle' or 'cat spring'. **Smalladine Copse** is a corruption of smael denu (small valley) and **Chambers Sale Copse** was named after Adam de la Chaumbre, who owned the land in the 13th century.

Porterswood Farm was named from John le Porter de Burcote (a 13th century owner) and **Sholebroke Lodge** is from sceald broc (shallow brook). **The Gullet** is from an old name for a gulley or ravine.

WICKEN

The word wicen was the Saxon plural of wic meaning a 'specialised farm'. There was just one village here in the 11th century, called Wicha, but later in the Middle Ages two separate settlements developed, divided by a stream. These were Wyke Dyve and Wyke Hamon. The former was owned by William de Dyve, the latter was owned by Hamon Filius Mainfelin. The two settlements were reunited in 1587 and this has been celebrated annually ever since.

Wicken Park was owned by Sir John Mordaunt in the early 19th century and later by Lord Penrhyn. It is now a private school.

Dagnall was Daggenhale in 1319, a corruption of Dagga's healh (nook or corner of land). This stands next to an abandoned course of the Great Ouse river.

WILBARSTON

Wilberteston in 1086 was Wilbeorht's tun (farmstead) but a later spelling, Wilberdestock in 1160, appears to have substituted a suffix from stocc (stump) perhaps because of the nearness of Stoke Albany.

Mill Yard is named after the steam-powered flour mill which once stood here, and in Barlows Lane is a row of cottages once called Workhouse Yard, of evident derivation.

South-eastwards is **Askershaw Wood** which was Asketeshawe in the Middle Ages, with a prefix from the personal name Asketiil and a suffix from haga (enclosure). **Barrowdykes Wood** is a corruption of bearu (woodland) and dic (ditch).

WILBY

This was the by (village) near the welig (willow tree) although some etymologists think the prefix comes instead from a personal name Willa. In the Domesday Book the village was Wilebi, a century later in 1186 it was Willebi.

The pub the **Horse Shoe** was once a blacksmith's shop. The Wilby Park mobile home site was formerly Wilby Lido, an open air swimming pool much enjoyed by the people of Wellingborough from the 1930s to the 1950s.

WINWICK

Winewican in 1043 and Winewiche in the 1086 Domesday Book were not far removed from the original form – Wina's wic (specialist farm). Later it became Wenewyk (1285) and Wyneweke (1416).

The local water meadows offered good pastures for cattle so the 'wic' here was probably a dairy farm.

WOLLASTON

Wulflaf's tun (farmstead) became Wilavastone by 1086 and Wurdlaueston by 1190. In the 13th century it was recorded as Wolaston.

Beacon Hill used to be called Mill Hill. It is the site of a Norman castle. **St Michael's Lane** is so named probably because it was here that the annual village fair took place, at Michaelmas. **College Street** was once called Backway.

Hardwater Mill is not named from the quality of its water, but from a crossing point here. It was once called Herdewath, or Hardewath, the suffix deriving from the Saxon waed (wading place). The ground under this ford was probably hard or firm. **Ryeholmes Bridge** was Ryeholm in 1337 – the holmr (marshy island) where rye was grown.

The nearby village of **Strixton** was Stric's tun (farmstead). In medieval times it was Strixtone and Strextone.

WOODFORD

Here the derivation is easily deduced: 'ford by the wood'. The Saxon word for 'wood' was wudu. In the Domesday Book the spelling was Wodeford, in 1403 it was Woddeford.

Hill House was the home of Henry Attehil in the Middle Ages. The **Dukes Arms** pub was once called the Lords Arms after the lord of the manor. The name was changed in honour of the Duke of Wellington, who used to come here for a drink whilst visiting his friend Charles Arbuthnot. For much of the 19th century the Arbuthnots lived at Woodford House, a little distance away towards Kettering. The road junction near the house is still known as 'Generals Corner'.

WOODFORD HALSE

From the original Wodeford in the 12th century (ford by the wood) this was given its present addendum in order to distinguish this village from the Woodford near Thrapston. Halse (near Brackley) was the manor to which the settlement belonged.

Up to the 19th century Woodford Halse was dominated by its larger neighbour, Hinton. But then the railways came. Soon a major junction appeared to the south and industries moved in, leading to some urban development. The lines have now disappeared but Woodford Halse keeps much of its railway character. There is still a Railway Club, a **Station Court** (a block of flats for the elderly) and a **Great Central Way**.

WOODNEWTON

The village once stood in the middle of the forest of King's Cliffe and was called Wodeneuton in 1255 to distinguish it from other Newton villages. Before then it was simply called Niwetone (1086) or Newinton (1166) – the neowe tun (new farm).

Priors Haw is derived from the fact that it was the haga (enclosure) owned by the Priors of Peterborough.

■ YARDLEY GOBION

This was Gerdeslai in 1166 and Jeardelegh in 1286, derived from gyrda (yards or poles) and leah (clearing), an area of woodland where poles were cut and made. By the 16th century the place had become Yardeley Gubbyn, the appendage coming from Henry Gubyun who held land here. Nearby **Gubbins Hill** preserves this old name and pronunciation.

Elm Green is named from an old elm tree, removed when the green was levelled in the 1970s.

Westwards is **Moor End**, a corruption of mor end meaning the 'end of the marsh'. Beyond is **Queens Oak**. Legend says this was where Edward IV first met Elizabeth Woodville, whom he later married, thus setting off the Wars of the Roses. The Woodvilles were lords of the neighbouring manor of Grafton Regis.

YARDLEY HASTINGS

This estate village was built by the Castle Ashby estate of the Marquess of Northampton, but the original settlement was just a small hamlet in the midst of Yardley Chase, the medieval hunting park. It was Gerdelai in 1086 and Jeredele in 1220 – probably derived from gyrda leah, the 'woodland clearing' where 'yards' or 'poles' were cut. In the late 13th century John de Hastings (Earl of Pembroke) became, by marriage to the Countess of Huntingdon, the lord of the manor. Subsequently the village gained its present appendage.

To the south is **Biggin Lodge** (a corruption of the Saxon bigging meaning 'building') close to which is **Cowper's Oak**. This is said to have been planted by William I's niece Judith and used by the poet William Cowper for shelter from a thunderstorm. Nearby is **Arniss Copse**, which comes from earn-hoh (eagle spur) and **Grimpsey Copse**, which was Grim's haeg (enclosure).

Blenley Farm was Blyndlye in the 16th century derived from blind leah (clearing), a clearing hidden from view perhaps. **Roundhay Farm** was Roundeheye in the 13th century – a circular haeg (enclosure).

YARWELL

Jarewelle (1166) and Yardewell (1316) were thought to come either from gear (fishing pool) and wielle (spring), or else from gearuwe (yarrow grass). The village stands by the Nene, where the river widens across the water meadows, so either derivation could be true.

Sulehay, near Wansford, was Sywleg in 1219, probably coming from Seofan leah – the clearing of the Seofa tribe.

YELVERTOFT

This was probably Geldfrith's toft (homestead). From Cevrecot in 1086 it became Gelvertoft (12th century) and Zelvertoft (14th century). The four lanes of the village, at right angles to the High Street, were named after long-dead farmers: **Ward**, **Tarry**, **Swinnerton** and **Ashwell**.

Speller Farm was Longespellowe in the 14th century, which meant 'long speech hill'. This was probably an ancient assembly point, being the place where many old trackways met.

Index

ABTHORPE 7
  Challock Farm 7
  Foscote 7
  Hayes Farm 7
ADDINGTON, Great Little 7
  Home Farm 8
  Shooters Hill 8
ADSTONE 8
ALDERTON 8
ALDWINCLE 9
  Bradshaw Wood 9
  Brancey Bridge 9
  Souther Wood 9
APETHORPE 9
  Halefield Lodge 9
ARTHINGWORTH 10
  Langborough Wood 10
  Waterloo Covert 10
ASHBY ST LEDGERS 10
  Stadfield 11
  Woolspit 11
ASHLEY 11
ASHTON 11
  Ashwood Farm 11
  Gun Hole 11
ASHTON (nr Oundle) 11
  Chapel Farm 12
  Chequered Skipper, The 12
ASTCOTE 12
  Dalscote 12
  Eastcote 12
  Grimscote 12
ASTON-LE-WALLS 13
  Welsh Road 13
AYNHO 13
  Butts, The 14
  Cartwright Arms, The 14
  College Farm 13
  Hollow Way 14
  Pesthouse Wood 13
  Port Way 14
  Smanhill Covert 13

BADBY 14
  Arbury Hill 14
  Knightley Way 14
BARBY 15
  Arnold Arms, The 15
  Chapel Farm 15
  Onley 15
BARNWELL 15
  Montagu Arms, The 15
  Wigsthorpe 15
BARTON SEAGRAVE 16
  Castle Way 16
  Gotch Road 16
  Ise, River 16
  Polwell Lane 16
BENEFIELD,
  Upper & Lower 17
BILLING, Great & Little 17
  Elwes Arms, The 17
  Elwes Way 17
  Knights Court 17

Lady Winefrides's Walk 17
BLAKESLEY 17
  Bartholomew Arms, The 18
  Dryden's Oak 18
  Woodend 18
BLATHERWYCKE 18
  Britain Sale 18
  Cadge Wood 18
  Hostage Wood 18
BLISWORTH 19
BODDINGTON, Upper &
  Lower 19
  Welsh Road 19
BOUGHTON 19
  Butchers Lane 20
  Whyte Melville, The 20
BOZEAT 20
  Allan Hill 21
  Burnt Close 20
  Dungee Woods 21
  Dychurch 21
  Top Road 21
BRACKLEY 21
  Allen Street 22
  Bannerman Street 22
  Bartlett Street 22
  Beaumont Street 22
  Bell, The 22
  Bridgewater Crescent 21
  Bridgewater Road 21
  Buckingham Road 22
  Cartwright Street 22
  Clarke Street 22
  Coles Street 22
  De Montfort Street 22
  De Quincey Street 22
  Egerton Close 22
  Ellesmere Estate 22
  Fenton Street 22
  Flora Thompson Drive 22
  Gardener Street 22
  Goose Green 22
  Halls Lane 22
  Halse 21
  Harrows, The 22
  Hawkins Street 22
  Hill Street 22
  Jones Street 22
  Locomotive, The 22
  Magdalen meadows 22
  Manor Court 21
  Manor Road 21
  Mill Lane 21
  Reindeer, The 22
  St James Road 22
  St Peter's Road 22
  St Rumbald's Well 21
  Soudan Avenue 22
  Spencer Street 22
  Spiers Street 22
  Stratton Street 22
  Water Lane 21
  Waynflete Avenue 22
  Waynflete Close 22

BRADDEN 23
  Bury Brake 23
BRAFIELD-ON-
  THE-GREEN 23
BRAMPTON ASH 23
  Hermitage, The 23
  Hermitage Road 23
  Hermitage Wood 23
BRAMPTON,
  Chapel & Church 24
  Hall Close 24
  Hoe Hill 24
  Merry Tom Lane 24
  Spencer Arms, The 24
  Spinney Farm 24
BRAUNSTON 25
  Berry Fields 25
  Boatman, The 25
  Dark Lane 25
BRAYBROOKE 25
  Eckland Lodge Farm 26
  Griffin Road 26
  Swan Inn, The 26
BRIGSTOCK 26
  Bocase Stone 26
  Hall Hill 26
  Kennel Hill 26
  Lyveden New Build 26
  Stable Hill 26
BRINGTON,
  Great & Little 27
  Althorp House 27
  Chinkwell 27
  Gawburrow Hill 27
  Moor Farm 27
  Nobottle 27
BRIXWORTH 27
  Coach and Horses, The 28
  Wolfage Piece 28
BROCKHALL 28
BROUGHTON 28
BUGBROOKE 29
  Bakers Arms, The 29
  Campion School 29
  Knitters Grave 29
BULWICK 29
  Henwick 29
BURTON LATIMER 29
  Buccleuch Farm 30
  Harper's Lodge 30
BYFIELD 30
  Becketts Close 30
  Cross Tree, The 30
  Edwards Close 30
  Fessey 30
  Fiveways 30
  Greenwood Close 30
  Jubilee Close 30
  Knightley Close 30
  Lovett Road 30
  Muddy Lane 30
  Thomas Close 30
  Welsh Rod 30
  Westhorpe 30

CANONS ASHBY 31
Conduit Covert 31
Wards Copse 31
CASTLE ASHBY 31
Chadstone 32
CATESBY,
Upper & Lower 32
Catwell Barn 32
Dane Hole 32
Ryton Hill 32
Steppington Hill 32
CHACOMBE 32
Bell Cottage 32
School Hill 32
Silver Street 32
Weavers Cottage 32
CHARLTON 33
Newbottle 33
CHARWELTON 33
Fox and Hounds, The 33
Foxhall Farm 33
CHELVESTON 34
Caldecott 34
CHIPPING WARDEN 34
Griffin, The 34
CLIPSTON 34
Longhold Lodge 34
Nobold Farm 34
Twantry Farm 34
CLOPTON 35
Long Thong Farm 35
Ringdales Wood 35
Skulking Dudley Copse 35
COGENHOE 35
COLD ASHBY 35
Chilcote's Cover 36
Portly Ford Bridge 36
COLD HIGHAM 36
Grimscote 36
Potcote 36
COLLINGTREE 36
COLLYWESTON 37
Cavalier, The 37
Deepside 37
New Road 37
CORBY 37
Excellent, Great &
Little 38
Jamb, The 37
Knights Lodge 37
Lloyds Road 38
Occupation Road 38
Pengreen Lane 38
Stockey Wood 38
COSGROVE 39
St Vincent's Well 39
COTON 39
Clay Coton 39
COTTERSTOCK 40
COTTESBROOKE 40
Calender Farm 40
Mitley Spinney 40
Monk's Well 40
St Norberts Field 40
COTTINGHAM 40
Great Cattage Wood 41
COURTEENHALL 41

CRANFORD 41
CRANSLEY,
Great & Little 41
Three Cranes, The 42
CREATON 42
Bricklayers Arms, The 42
Horseshoe Inn 42
CRICK 42
Boat Horse Lane 43
Lauds Road 43
Phoenix House 43
Queen's House 43
CROUGHTON 43
College Farm 43
Rowler Farm 43
CULWORTH 44
Berry Hill 44
Fulford Farm 44
King Charles' Pebble 44
Wadground Barn 44

DAVENTRY 44
Abbey Street 45
Borough Hill 45
Brook Street 46
Burnt Walls 45
Daintree Farm 45
Daintry Wood 45
Drayton 45
Falconershill 45
Fousill Wood 45
Hackwood Farm 45
Middlemore Farm 45
New Street 46
Newlands 46
North Street 46
Oxford Street 46
Petty Cury 46
Pyghties, The 46
St John's Square 46
Sheaf Street 46
Stepnell Spinney 45
Tavern Lane 46
DEANSHANGER 46
Ashalls Copse 47
Dove House Farm 47
Dukes Head, The 47
Little London 47
Puxley 47
Redmoor Copse 47
Woodman's Arms, The 47
DEENE 47
Deenethorpe 47
DENFORD 48
DENTON 48
DESBOROUGH 49
Buckwell Close 49
Compton Street 49
Havelock Street 49
King Street 49
New Street 49
Queen Street 49
Regent Street 49
Union Street 49
Victoria Street 49
DINGLEY 49
DODFORD 50

DUDDINGTON 50
Assart Farm 50
Dales Wood 50
DUSTON 51
Hopping Hill, The 51
Melbourne Arms, The 51
Melbourne Lane 51

EARLS BARTON 51
Berry Mount 51
Boot, The 52
Dowthorpe End 51
Syke Way 51
EAST CARLTON 52
EAST FARNDON 52
Judith Stone 52
EASTON MAUDIT 52
EASTON NESTON 53
EASTON-ON-THE-HILL 53
Exeter Arms, The 53
Neville Day Close 53
Vigo Lodge 53
ECTON 54
Three Horseshoes, The 54
Worlds End Inn, The 54
EDGCOTE 54
Danes Moor 55
Paddle Cottage 55
ELKINGTON 55
Cot Hill 55
Honey Hill 55
EVENLEY 56
Astwick 56
Plowman's Furze 56
EVERDON,
Great & Little 56
Everdon Stubbs 57
Mantles Heath 57
Snorescombe 56
Westcombe 56
EYDON 57
Manitoba Estate, The 57
FARTHINGHOE 57
Coleready Farm 57
Ouse Well 57
Steane 57
FARTHINGSTONE 58
Joymead 58
FAWSLEY 58
Kingbrook Spinney 58
FINEDON 58
Debdale Grove 59
Mulso Arms, The 59
Mulso Road 59
Ryebury Hill 59
FINESHADE 59
Lynn Wood 59
Westhay Wood 59
FLORE 59
Adams Cottage 59
Glassthorpehill 60
FOTHERINGHAY 60
Castle Farm 61
Walcot Lodge 61

GAYTON 61
Eykyn Arms, The 61

Millmott 61
GEDDINGTON 61
Brand, Great & Little 62
Langley Quarter 62
Rising Bridge 62
Sart Wood 62
Wood Street 61
GLAPTHORN 62
Provost Lodge 62
GRAFTON REGIS 63
Queen's Oak 63
GRAFTON
UNDERWOOD 63
Grafton Park Wood 63
GREAT DODDINGTON 64
Cut-Throat Lane 64
Doddington Manor
Farm 64
GREAT OXENDEN 64
GREATWORTH 64
Cockley Brake 65
Dering Cottages 65
Westhorp 65
GREENS NORTON 65
Caswell 65
Duncote 65
Field Burcote 65
Kingsthorn Wood 65
Plumton 65
GRENDON 65
GRETTON 66
Hatton Arms, The 66
Kirby Hall 66
Presgrave Copse 66
Talbot, The 66
Thatchams Copse 66
GUILSBOROUGH 67
Lindow Spinney 67
Nortoft Lodge &
Grange 67
Ward Arms, The 67

HACKLETON 67
HADDON, East & West 68
Hungerwell Barn 68
Oster Hill 68
HANNINGTON 68
Hannington Grange 68
HARDINGSTONE 69
Basin, The 69
Rouse Corner 69
HARDWICK 69
HARGRAVE 70
HARLESTONE 70
Dudman's Plantation 70
Fleetland Farm 70
Harlestone Heath 70
Sowditch Thicket 70
HARPOLE 70
Blackwell's Farm 71
Flitnell Barn 71
HARRINGTON 71
Hospital Farm 71
Loatland 71
Newbottle Bridge 71
Nunnery Farm 71
Thorpe Underwood 71

Tollemache Arms, The 71
Wharf Lodge 71
HARRINGWORTH 72
Turtle Bridge 72
White Swan, The 72
HARROWDEN,
Great & Little 72
Furnace Lane 72
Ten O'Clock, The 72
HARTWELL 72
Chapel Farm 73
Rowley Wood 73
Salcey Forest 73
HASELBECH 73
HELLIDON 73
Attlefield Barn 73
Stockwell Lane 73
HELMDON 74
Astwell 74
Falcutt 74
Grange Farm 74
Stockings Farm 74
HEMINGTON 75
Beaulieu 75
Ellands Farm 75
HEYFORD,
Nether & Upper 75
Forester' Arms, The 75
Furnace Lane 75
Horestone Brook 75
HIGHAM FERRERS 76
Andrew Close 76
Anne Close 76
Charles Close 76
Chichele Close 76
College Street 76
Duchy Close 76
Duchy Farm 76
Edward Close 76
Elizabeth Way 76
John White Close 77
Lancaster Farm 76
Lancaster Street 76
Midland Road 76
Saffron Moat 76
Saffron Road 76
Vine Hill Drive 76
Windmill Banks 76
HINTON 77
Warden Grange 77
West Farndon 77
HINTON-IN-
THE-HEDGES 77
Crewe Arms, The 77
HOLCOT 78
HOLDENBY 78
Delf Spinney 78
Kings Walk 78
Twigden Spinney 78
HOLLOWELL 78
HORTON 79
Cheyney Farm 79
HOUGHTON,
Great & Little 79
Clifford Hill 79

IRCHESTER 80

Arkwright Estate 81
Knuston Hall 80
Wembley Pit 80
IRTHLINGBOROUGH 81
College Street 81
Coneygears 82
Ditchford Mill 81
Hayway Estate 81
John Pyel Road 81
New Street 81
Station Road 81
ISHAM 82
Ise, River 82
Manor Farm 82
ISLIP 82

KELMARSH 83
Shipley Wood 83
KETTERING 83
Alfred Street 85
Belfry Lane 85
Buccleuch, The 86
Buccleuch Street 84
Carey Mission House 86
Carey Street 86
Cordwainer, The 86
Dalkeith Place 84
Dryland Street 86
Duke Street 84
Field Street Avenue 85
Fuller Church 86
Fuller Street 86
Gold Street 85
Gotch Road & Close 85
Headlands 84
Horse Market 85
Huxloe Place 84
Knibb Centre 86
Knibb Street 86
Leathercraftsman, The 86
Lindsay Street 86
Links Lodge 84
Lower Street 85
Market Street 85
Meadow Road 85
Mikado Pheasant, The 86
Montgu Street 84
Northall Street 84
Rockingham Road 84
Sawyer's Almshouses 86
Sheep Street 85
Silver Street 85
Tanners Lane 85
Toller Chapel 86
Toller Place 86
Upper Field Street 85
Wadcroft 84
Walker Lane 85
Wicksteed Park 83
KILSBY 87
Devon Ox Road 87
Essen Lane 87
Manor Road 87
Middle Street 87
Smarts Estate 87
KINGS CLIFFE 87
Buxton Wood 88

Calvey Wood 88
Cornforth Homes 88
Law's Lawn 88
Old Warren, The 88
Setehill 88
Stockings 88
Westhay Wood 88
KINGS SUTTON 89
Astrop 89
Butchers Arms, The 89
Lovells 89
Port Way 89
Purston 89
Red Lion Street 89
St Rumbalds Well 89
Twyford Farm 89
Walton Grounds 89
Whittall Street 89
KISLINGBURY 90
Bly Lane 90
Cromwell Cottage 90
Hill Farm 90
Hollowell Hill Farm 90
Stockall Farm 90

LAMPORT 91
Faxton 91
Hanging Houghton 91
Lamport Swan, The 91
LAXTON 91
Spanhoe Farm 91
Spanhoe Wood 91
LILBOURNE 92
Dow Bridge 92
LILFORD 92
Lilford Owl, The 92
LITCHBOROUGH 92
Radmore Farm 92
LODDINGTON 93
Orton 93
LONG BUCKBY 93
Cotton End 93
Greenhill Farm 94
Holborough Hill 93
Leighton Lodge 94
Murcott 94
Rockhall Hill 94
Ryehill Lodge 94
Surney 93
LOWICK 94
Bullicks Wood 94
Drayton House 94
Germain Rooms 94
Lowick Oak 94
Oxen Wood 94
LUDDINGTON-IN-
THE-BROOK 94
LUTTON 95
Papley 95

MAIDFORD 95
Burntfold Copse 95
MAIDWELL 96
Berrydale Covert 96
Loder Hall 96
Manor Farm 96
St Peter's Close 96

Scotland Wood 96
MARSTON ST
LAWRENCE 96
Costow House 96
Dean Barn 96
Marston Yew 96
MARSTON TRUSSELL 96
Cavaliers Grave 97
MEARS ASHBY 97
Griffins Head, The 97
MIDDLETON 97
Swinawe Wood 98
Yokewood Lodge 98
MIDDLETON CHENEY 98
Halt, The 98
Moors Drive 98
Overthorpe 98
MILTON MALSOR 98
MORETON PINKNEY 99
Canada 99
Plumpton 99
MOULTON 99
Artichoke, The 99
Thorpelands 99

NASEBY 100
Avon Well 100
Fitzgerald Arms, The 100
Gynwell 100
Prince Rupert's Farm 100
Shuckburgh Farm 100
NASSINGTON 100
Great Byards Sale 100
Lyveden Farm 101
NEWNHAM 101
Butts Ley 101
Codwell Spring 101
Coppid Moor Spring 101
Horns Lane 101
Langhill Spring 101
Manor Lane 101
Mounts Lane 101
Narbrook Spring 101
Parkins Way 101
Romer Arms, The 101
School Hill 101
NEWTON 102
Barford Lodge 102
NEWTON
BROMSWOLD 102
NORTHAMPTON 102
Abbey Street 104
Abbots Way 104
Abington 103
Angel Lane 106
Beakward Street 106
Beckets Park 105
Beckets Well 105
Booth Lane 103
Boothville 103
Borough, The 104
Bull and Butcher,
The 106
Castle Lane 103
Cherry Orchard
Estate 103
Clicker, The 106

College Street 106
Cotton End 103
Cotton End Mill 105
Delapre 103
Derngate 106
Drapery, The 105
Far Cotton 103
Franklins Gardens 105
Garibaldi, The 106
Gold Street 105
Grey Friars Bus
Station 104
Horse Market 106
Hunsbury Hill 104
King Billy, The 106
Kingsley 103
Kingsthorpe 103
Lumbertubs 104
Mailcoach, The 106
Mare Fair 106
Mercers Row 105
Newland 106
Nunn Mills 105
Paddy's Meadow 104
Parade, The 106
Peveril Way 104
Princess Alexandra,
The 106
Red Rover, The 106
Rushmere 103
St James district 104
St James End Mill 105
Semi-Long 104
Sheep Street 106
Tanner Street 106
Weston Favell 103
Wood Hill 106
Woolmonger Street 106
NORTON 107
Mazedale Spinney 107
Muscott 107
Noborough Farm 107
Tattle Bank Row 107
Thrupp Grounds 107

OAKLEY, Great & Little 108
Carlton Purlieus 108
Monks Well 108
Oakley Purlieus 108
OLD 108
OLD STRATFORD 108
Chapel Close 109
Shrobb Lodge Farm 109
Windmill Field 109
ORLINGBURY 109
Badsaddle Wood 109
OUNDLE 109
Herne Road 110
Latham Way 110
New Street 110
North Street 110
St Osyth's Lane 110
Ship Lane 110
Talbot Hotel 110
West Street 110
Wyatt Way 110
OVERSTONE 110

PASSENHAM 111
  Boswell Lane 111
  Church Lane 111
  Folly Lane 111
  Patrick's Lane 111
  St Guthlac's Church 111
  Shrob Walk 111
PATTISHALL 111
  Debdale Flats 112
  Fosters Booth 112
PAULERSPURY 112
  Cuttle Mill 112
  Heathencote 112
  Plumpton End 112
  Pury End 112
  Stockings Field 112
  Tews End 112
PIDDINGTON 112
PILTON 113
  Bearshank Wood 113
  Winning Foot Hill 113
PIPEWELL 113
  Monks Arbour Wood 113
  Rawshaw Wood 113
PITSFORD 114
  Griffin, The 114
POLEBROOK 114
  Armston 114
  Burray Spinney 114
  Coney Geer Coppice 114
  Kingsthorpe Lodge 114
POTTERSPURY 115
  Blackwell End 115
  Brownswood Cottage 115
  Cock, The 115
  Furtho 115
  Old Talbot, The 115
  Wakefield 115
PRESTON CAPES 115
  Cleaver's Clump 116
  Portway 116
PYTCHLEY 116
  Cox's 'Lodge 116
  Isham Road 116
  Overstone Arms, The 116

QUINTON 117

RADSTONE 117
  Coldharbour Farm 117
RAUNDS 117
  Butts Road 118
  Darsdale 118
  Knighton's Row 118
  Midland Road 118
  Mullows Cotton 118
  Station Road 118
  Worlde Upside Down,
    The 118
RAVENSTHORPE 118
RINGSTEAD 118
ROADE 119
  Thorpewood Farm 119
ROCKINGHAM 119
  Sondes Arms, The 119
ROTHERSTHORPE 120
  Berry/Bury, The 120

Brook Farm 120
Chequers, The 120
ROTHWELL 121
  Castle Hill 121
  Crispin Street 121
  John Smith Avenue 122
  Ponder Street 122
  Ragsdale Street 121
  Shotwell Mill Lane 121
  Sun Hill 121
  Tresham Street 121
  Well Lane 121
RUSHDEN 122
  College Street 122
  Crabb Street 122
  Denton Close 123
  Duck Street 122
  Fitzwilliam Street 123
  George Street 123
  Newton Road 122
  Pemberton Street 122
  Rectory Road 122
  Sartoris Road 122
  Spencer Road 123
  Tollbar 123
RUSHTON 123
  Gaultney Wood 124
  Storefield 124
  Thornhill Arms, The 124
  Triangular Lodge 124

SCALDWELL 124
  Roseholm 124
SIBBERTOFT 125
  Castle Yard 125
  Dust Hill 125
  Moot Hill 125
  Sulby 125
  Westhorpe Lane 122
SILVERSTONE 125
  Abbey Curve 126
  Becket's Corner 126
  Challock Farm 126
  Chapel Curve 126
  Copse Corner 126
  Maggotts Drive 126
SLAPTON 126
SLIPTON 126
SOUTHWICK 126
  Blackmore Thick
    Farm 127
  Crayley Wood 127
  Morehay Lawn 127
  Old Sale 127
  Park Colsters 127
  Perio Mill 127
  Shuckburgh Arms,
    The 127
  Tottenhoe Lodge 127
SPRATTON 127
  Broomhill 127
  Teeton 128
STANFORD-ON-
  AVON 128
  Downtown 128
STANION 128
  Cardigan Arms, The 128

'Corby Haw 129
Cowthick 129
STANWICK 129
  Dolben Avenue 129
  Duke of Wellington,
    The 129
STAVERTON 129
  Elderstubbs Farm 130
  Studborough Hill 129
STOKE ALBANY 130
STOKE BRUERNE 130
  Shutlanger 131
STOKE DOYLE 131
  Hatchdoyle 131
  Shuckburgh Arms,
    The 131
STOWE IX CHURCHES 131
  Ramsden Corner
    Plantation 132
SUDBOROUGH 132
  Money Holes 132
  Round Lown Wood 132
  Vane Arms, The 132
SULGRAVE 132
  Barrow Hill 132
  Park Lane 133
  Stockwell Lane 133
SUTTON BASSETT 133
SYRESHAM 133
  Abbey Way 134
  Earls Wood 134
  Hoppersford Farm 134
  Monks Wood 134
  Shiplands Copse 134
  Wetley's Wood 134
SYWELL 134
  Hayes Lodge 134

TANSOR 134
THENFORD 135
THORPE MALSOR 135
THORPE MANDEVILLE 135
  Bull's Lane 135
  Doctors Close 135
  Dove Close 135
  Ox-Yard 135
THORPE WATERVILLE 136
  Achurch 136
  Linches, The 136
  Thorpe Achurch 136
THRAPSTON 136
  Cedar Drive 137
  Chancery Lane 136
  De Vere Road 136
  Gales Lodge 137
  Midland Road 136
  Oakleas Drive 137
  Oundle Road 136
TITCHMARSH 137
  Bidwell Farm 137
  Chequer Hill Coppice 137
  Coales Lodge 137
  Polopit 137
TOWCESTER 137
  Brave Old Oak, The 138
  Bury Mount 138
  Caldecote 138

Costwell Farm 138
Easton Neston House 138
Folly, The 138
Gilbert Scott Court 138
Handley 138
Hulcote 138
Malt House Court 138
Nun Wood 138
Pomfret Arms, The 138
Pomfret Road 138
Showsley Grounds 138
TWYWELL 139
Blackwells Close 139

WADENHOE 139
WAKERLEY 139
Exeter Arms, The 139
WALGRAVE 140
Hall Farm 140
WANSFORD 140
Haycock Hotel, The 140
WAPPENHAM 140
Blackmires Farm 140
Cockerell's Copse 140
Potash Farm 140
Radmore Farm 140
WARKTON 141
WARKWORTH 141
Franklow Knob Farm 141
Grimsbury 141
Huscote 141
Nethercote 141
Spital Farm 141
WARMINGTON 141
Davey's Farm 142
Eaglethorpe 141
Stock Hill 142
WATFORD 142
Burnums Farm 142
Langborough 142
Rodmore Lodge 142
Silsworth Lodge 142
WEEDON BEC 142
WEEDON LOIS 143
Milthorpe 143
WEEKLEY 143
Boughton House 143
Weekley Hall Wood 143
WELDON,
Great & Little 144
Bangrave Wood 144
Priors Hall 144
WELFORD 144
Hemploe Lodge 144
Hemplow Hills 144
Wharf House, The 144
WELLINGBOROUGH 144
Abbey Road 145

Abbots Way 145
Albert Road 147
Alexandra Road 147
Appleby Gate 146
Askham Avenue 146
Brickhill Road 147
Brook Farm 146
Brookfield 145
Buckwell 145
Butlins Sidings 147
Castle Fields 146
Castle Lane 146
Castle Mews 146
Castle Road 146
Chace Road 147
Cherry Avenue 147
Chester Road 147
Colwell Road 147
Croyland Park 145
Dulley Avenue 147
Friars Close 145
Hatton House 146
Hatton Park 146
Havelock Street 147
Herriots Lane 145
Hill Street 145
Hind Hotel 146
Holly Well 145
Lady Well 145
Mannock Road 146
Midland Road 147
Monks Way 145
Newcomen Road 147
Pinder Road 146
Plumtree Avenue 147
Priory Road 145
Pyghtle 147
Red Well 145
Rock Street 145
St John Street 145
Senwick Road 147
Spring Gardens 145
Spring Hill 145
Stanley Road 147
Stone Well 145
Swanpool 145
Victoria Road 147
Vivian Road 146
Well Street 145
Whyte Well 145
WELTON 147
Cockle Farm 148
Hobberhill Farm 147
Mickle Way 148
WESTON 148
Armada House 148
WESTON-BY-
WELLAND 148

Wheel and Compass,
The 148
WHILTON 148
WHISTON 149
WHITFIELD 149
WHITTLEBURY 149
Cattlehill Wood 149
Chambers Sale Copse 149
Gullet, The 150
Porterswood Farm 150
Sholebroke Lodge 150
Smalladine Copse 149
WICKEN 150
Dagnall 150
WILBARSTON 150
Askershaw Wood 150
Barrowdykes Wood 150
Mill Yard 150
WILBY 151
Horse Shoe, The 151
WINWICK 151
WOLLASTON 151
Beacon Hill 151
College Street 151
Hardwater Mill 151
Ryeholomes Bridge 151
St Michael's Lane 151
Strixton 151
WOODFORD 152
Dukes Arms, The 152
Hill House 152
WOODFORD HALSE 152
Great Central Way 152
Station Court 152
WOODNEWTON 152
Priors Haw 152

YARDLEY GOBION 153
Elm Green 153
Gubbins Hill 153
Moor End 153
Queens Oak 153
YARDLEY HASTINGS 154
Arniss Copse 154
Biggin Lodge 154
Blenley Farm 154
Cowper's Oak 154
Grimpsey Copse 154
Roundhay Farm 154
YARWELL 154
Sulehay 154
YELVERTOFT 155
Ashwell Lane 155
Speller Farm 155
Swinnerton Lane 155
Tarry Lane 155
Ward Lane 155